WIN INSIDE TO WIN OUTSIDE

Uncover Your Purpose, Identify Your Natural Passions, Remove Barriers, and Achieve Unstoppable Success with a New Mindset

Azarudeen M J

connect2azarudeen@gmail.com

Thank you for purchasing this book!

As a token of appreciation, I would like to share a valuable gift with you : "**Learn 4 key Strategies to Showcase Your Value Differentiation**". Please claim your gift by using the following link:

https://azarudeen-mj.ck.page/f46f7974be

Creating value differentiation means developing unique skills, expertise, or approaches that make them indispensable in their roles.

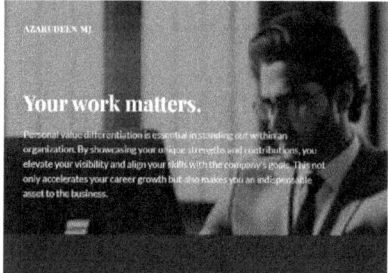

It's about standing out by delivering exceptional results, solving problems creatively, and consistently adding value beyond what is expected.

Without value differentiation, both professionals and businesses risk blending into the crowd, losing opportunities for growth, and failing to reach their full potential.

Ultimately, the key to sustained success lies in being known for something uniquely valuable, whether that's in your career or your business.

Table of content

Chapter 1: Introduction 6

The Real Winning: The Sculptor and the Stone. 6

What's the Secret to Winning? 9

Where Does Consistent Winning Begin? 9

The Foundation of Success: Building the Right Mindset 10

The Elephant's Story: Believe to Break Through 11

Your Purpose for Winning 13

Reality 18

What Can This Book Give You? 20

Chapter 2: The Catalyst to Kickstart Your Transformation 29

Stop, Think Deeply, Reprioritize, Replan and Repositioning yourself 29

Get to Know Your Real Personal Power 36

Brain Suspension Trick and Your Simple Game Plan 40

Precious Assets 42

Taken for Granted and Innocence 43

Contribution Requirement at Initial Phase 45

Imagination of The Best Version 46

Chapter 3: Barrier Stones to Self-Discovery: Unlocking the New You 51

Limiting Belief 51

Why Don't We Question Our Current Belief System? 57

Unconscious Impact of External Forces 59

A Story About Managing Self 64

Your Younger Version 66

Life of Animal 67

Getting to know about people's reality 68

The Journey Towards the Center of a Better Relationship 71

How Do You Keep Self-Motivated When You Are Completely Down? 74

Impact Your Value at Scale with Compassion . 77

Making a Small Difference to A Few Matters! . 77

Forgiveness is the Key to Success 78

Chapter 4: Clarity—How to Choose a Topic? 85

10 Ways to Identification of Your Topic 85

What Is the Source of Motivation For a Few Well-known Personalities? 101

A Research Study Outcome 106

The Transformation from Consumer to Creator Mindset 109

Branding the Authenticity [Identity Creation] 111

How does Identity Create a Brand and Boost Self-Confidence? *114*

Chapter 5: Setting up Internal Infrastructure.... 118

The Brain Exercises to Break the Pattern and Create New Neural Pathways *118*

Pause to Generate New Energy and Remove Brain Toxic Technique *120*

Sleep to Repair Technique *122*

14 Secrets to Prepare Winning Mindset *124*

Conclusion 137

May I ask you for a small favor? 139

Full Book Summary 140

Short Preview of My Upcoming Book in this Self Improvement Mastery Series 156

Chapter 1: Introduction

****

"What lies behind us and what lies before us are tiny matters compared to what lies within us."

— Ralph Waldo Emerson

The Real Winning: The Sculptor and the Stone

There was once a famous sculptor named Leo, renowned for creating lifelike statues from ordinary stone. One day, a young man approached him, eager to learn the art.

"Master, how do you carve such perfect statues?" the young man asked. Leo smiled and replied, "The secret is not in the stone, but in seeing the statue within it."

After carefully observing Leo's technique, the young man was eager to begin. He started chiselling away at a block of stone, but his efforts resulted in a jagged surface. Frustration and doubt crept in as he approached Leo, discouraged. "I can't see the statue you talked about. The stone won't take shape."

Leo responded, "First, you must see the statue within the stone. Then, simply remove everything that doesn't belong."

Intrigued yet confused, the young man followed Leo to a large block of stone. Leo explained, "This stone represents the outer world—your struggles, challenges, and everything you think you need to conquer. If you focus only on the outside, you'll never create something meaningful.

Change your perspective: look at the beauty of the statue and admire what is visible inside. Once you do, you'll easily identify the unwanted pieces to remove."

Understanding the struggle, Leo added, "The stone resists because you're holding on to your own doubts, impatience, and fear of failure. Just as the stone hides the statue, these inner struggles block your vision. Remove the excess within yourself first—your fear and need for perfection. Only then will the statue reveal itself."

Realizing that his true battle was not with the stone but with himself, the young man began to focus on his inner self. Gradually, as he let go of his doubts and impatience, the statue began to take shape.

In the end, he understood that the greatest masterpiece he sculpted was not the statue—but himself.

Moral of the Story: If you can't control your inner world, no amount of skill or talent will suffice when life shakes your foundation. True victory begins within. By approaching life with a genuine purpose—much like recognizing the beauty of a statue hidden within a block of stone—and maintaining a broader vision fueled by passion, you'll remain steady, no matter how the environment changes.

Effect of winning

Winning gives us a thrill—a surge of confidence and a momentary high. But with that high comes a subtle fear: how do we keep winning? People rarely want to hear about failures; they're captivated by success stories. When someone wins, others are eager to know their journey, their strategies, and their "winning formula." But why is everyone so drawn to winning? It's because winning offers so much: self-esteem, identity, a sense of worth, happiness, new networks, and often, financial security.

However, winning is not a permanent state. It's a journey. People often think winning is difficult—and they're right, but only if you're unprepared. Everyone strives for success, but only a few achieve it. Why is that?

Think of it like visiting a new city. On your first visit, you rely heavily on maps or directions, constantly seeking guidance. But after a few weeks, you begin to navigate the streets effortlessly. What changed? You've trained your brain, built a mental map, and gained confidence over time. Winning is much the same—it's about preparation and mental conditioning. The more you train, the easier it becomes. Without preparation, winning becomes an uphill battle.

What's the Secret to Winning?

Is it hard work? Partly, yes—but that's not the whole story. Before you even attempt to win, you must prepare your mind. What does that mean? It means developing a winning mindset before achieving any real victory.

It's like directing a movie. Before filming begins, the director has already visualized each scene in their mind. The plan, strategy, execution, and outcome have already played out in their imagination.

Similarly, every product we use today was once someone's imagination. The creator imagined it over and over, refining the idea before making it real. Just like that, building a winning mindset is key to success, even before the real win happens. So, precision in your internal victory ensures a higher rate of external success.

Where Does Consistent Winning Begin?

Let's consider a competition. The goal is to reach the target and outperform your competition. When it's your first attempt, there's mystery, doubt, and a series of unexpected obstacles. But with persistence, practice, and focus, you overcome those challenges and reach your goal. The feeling of that first win is exhilarating.

Now, imagine entering the same competition again. You already know the path to victory, and it feels more comfortable than before. But here's the catch: your focus may not be as sharp. You could lose, even with experience, because there are new competitors with the same intensity and hunger you had during your first attempt.

The key to consistent winning is to approach every challenge with the mindset of a first timer—always prepared, always innovating. You can't let the victory get to your head.

The Foundation of Success: Building the Right Mindset

Success is not just about skill. It's about consistency— about constantly improving and practicing. To be truly consistent, you must first break through the mental barriers that hold you back.

As *Albert Schweitzer* once said,

"Success is not the key to happiness. Happiness is the key to success. If you love what you are doing, you will be successful."

So, why do so many people settle for an ordinary life, never trying to win? The pressure of maintaining success can be overwhelming. When you win, people expect you to keep winning. The weight of those expectations can be daunting. On the flip side, losing brings its own challenges—fear of judgment, loss of respect, and self-doubt, to name a few.

But everyone should strive to win, not just for themselves, but for their loved ones and communities. This book will guide you with practical strategies on how to live a balanced, fulfilling life while maintaining a winning mindset.

Before we dive in, let me share some surprising truths about the world around you—and more importantly, about yourself. Understanding your **purpose** for winning is crucial. Once you are clear on the purpose, the strategies and mental preparation required to achieve it become much more apparent. The deeper your understanding of both, the easier it becomes to succeed. Throughout this book, I will guide you through these concepts step by step.

So, welcome aboard! **Winning yourself is the foundation of winning others**. Let's get started...

The Elephant's Story: Believe to Break Through

Once, a man was passing by an elephant camp and noticed that the huge adult elephants were tied to small trees with thin ropes. His surprise grew as he wondered why these strong animals didn't break free. Overwhelmed by his curiosity, he inquired with the caretaker, "How come these massive elephants never try to uproot the small tree or break the flimsy rope?" and they have the power to do so. An adult elephant can even fight a lion and win!"

The trainer smiled for a moment and said, "When elephants were young, we tied them with these thin ropes. At that age, they tried to break free but couldn't because they were not strong enough. As they grew, they became conditioned to believe that they couldn't break the rope, even though they now have the strength to do so."

The lesson from this story is about the power of the mind. Like elephants, we are conditioned to believe in certain limits. We never think of breaking free, even when we have the power to do so!

Our minds can either trap us in limiting beliefs or free us to achieve great things. Our past failures do not determine our future lives. As Albert Einstein said, imagination is key. If you picture yourself as this elephant right now, you may feel stuck in your old self with long-held beliefs. However, if you imagine yourself as a powerful, mighty elephant, you can completely find a person with NEW MINDSET now. Let's dive in and explore how to achieve this transformation.

Your Purpose for Winning

Your current state of being in this life is a reflection of the choices that have led you to this position. All right! After reaching a specific stage, most individuals opt to settle into a monotonous and uneventful routine for an extended period without questioning their current lifestyle, as they are unaware of being trapped in a pattern and miss out on fulfilling life.

I am filled with excitement knowing that you are lucky enough to avoid being among them. You have already made a wake-up call not to miss out on the opportunity to find your purpose in life. This book is your first step. Together, let's uncover the secrets to living a truly complete and fulfilling life. This life does not confine to any boundaries, but it needs to be filled with a diverse range of positive emotions and achievements.

It offers exponential growth, exhilarating excitement, deep satisfaction, lasting happiness, resounding success, mental abundance, unwavering pride, undeniable fulfillment, and an abundance of both health and wealth. All these incredible elements eagerly await your permission. Are you prepared to welcome these valuable assets?

Your current routine does not bring new success. Your life movie has YOU as the chief director. The script is all yours. You have the power to define your own characteristics, shaping them into who you want to be.

What about rewriting this manuscript to experience the unseen deep joy, success, and fulfillment, enabling you to escape from the ordinary to extraordinary life?

We are in an amazing era. We find ourselves in an overwhelming amount of information and data constantly surrounds us at every turn, which greatly influences and shapes the course of our existence. Technology made it possible to access any information at any time. The mega emergence of artificial intelligence gives us more than we imagined and simplifies our lives nowadays. In the early days, say nearly two decades back, accessing information and data was complex and needed much effort.

The Internet revolutionized our lives, facilitating communication, banking, travel, finance, and other activities. During this significant transformation, we constantly float in the vast ocean of daily survival, desperately seeking balance to sustain us.

Striking a balance between these various responsibilities can keep you constantly engaged, following a structured routine that encompasses waking up, working, or handling business affairs, meeting obligations, returning home, caring for others, spending time in front of screens, sleeping, and repeating the same cycle day in and day out.

In this routine, you care about your surroundings, such as family, friends, and belongings to comfort them, make them feel good. Whether you prefer it or not, the people around you constantly keep you occupied. Sometimes, you can't even recall how efficiently you managed your time last week. Your actions focus on meeting the needs of those closest to you, ensuring their well-being comes first. You always prioritize their needs and happiness over everything else. Your job or business commitment takes up all your time on the other side, leaving little room for anything else in your daily routine. Routine confines life within monotonous boundaries.

Have you ever thought to press a **PAUSE** button from these bustling rhythms and ask a few mindful questions?

> Have I ever tried to establish a connection with my inner self and uncover their genuine wants and aspirations?

> What brings me a greater sense of meaning, pride, happiness, and fulfillment?

> What belief is holding back from experiencing remarkable growth?

> Have I ever pondered my purpose, wondering what is the reason for my existence?

What transformation happened in my life in the past decade, which flew by?

Do I ever pause to reflect on my profound self-love and the life I currently lead?

What are the exciting factors that inspire me to wake up each morning?

Am I taking steps towards achieving the life I've always dreamt of?

How much do I know about myself (my strengths and weaknesses)?

When was the most recent occasion that I reflected on my life and documented it in my journal?

Have I ever taken the initiative to approach my family, friends, and colleagues and ask for their valuable feedback?

Did I ever try to work on or understand the meaning of feedback?

Or Am I just mindlessly continuing with my same daily routine?
Have I ever thought about making a small difference for future generations?

What is the daily time commitment needed to prioritize my intellectual well-being?

Looking at life from a different perspective helps to give a deeper meaning of your existence and path to meaningful and happy life. But it is not easy to answer this question. You know, every one of us will get these questions at some point in time or later part of their lives when mentally and physically struck somewhere. This is not the right approach to find the meaning of life. There is a better way to find it early. Let's move on to find it.

You are here not by accident. There is a strong purpose behind it. Nature compels you to awaken and eagerly expects your actions in pursuit of this profound purpose. Please understand that I am not attempting to preach about spiritual life. I want to help you live a life filled with fulfillment, finding joy within yourself, and finding meaning in every action can be just as transformative as having a spiritual journey.

The key is to discover your true passion and purpose early on and fully engage with life's experiences and sensations. This will quickly

take you to achieve financial independence and fulfillment. It doesn't matter how long you've missed out; today is the best day to start. Congratulations, you're already on your way now!

Reality

Small wins in work, such as promotions or minor business successes, provide short moments of satisfaction. However, this happiness is fleeting, and soon after, you feel emptiness and start searching for the next target, driven by your environment. This endless cycle of seeking temporary satisfaction and proving your status never truly fulfills you.

Your entire life revolves around these short-lived excitements. After each small win, you are back to square one with emptiness. I call this the "cycle of emptiness". Always wanting something more and never satisfied mindset. This becomes a routine habit. Almost 80% of our lifetime is stuck in this state, causing us to forget to embrace the present joyful moments.

Unless you make time to think and reflect on the above questions, the cycle of emptiness will persist. During my research, I have asked these questions to different individuals. In addition, I was curious to know the answer to the following question: "What is your ultimate purpose or goal in life?" The responses included: "Hmmmm…I never really thought about it,"

"My life goal is simply to be happy," and "To explore the world once I've attained financial security."

Unfortunately, there were no thoughtful answers, and it seemed that the question felt very odd to them. However, I was sure my questions provoked them to think about something they had never considered before.

Besides this, a few more questions, like, "How did you plan to live happily? If something goes wrong and you lose your hard earnings and savings, will you continue to be happy?" No answers or no plan. What is the real problem here? Many people prioritize gaining physical possessions, neglecting the opportunity to explore their self-worth within this trap. However, while assets hold significance in life, they are not the sole determining factor of importance. Money cannot be used to buy true happiness and satisfaction.

If someone requested you to introduce yourself, what would you say about yourself as a remarkable person? Is it possible to list down any or one heart-fulfilling achievement without including certificates or professional or business achievements?

Have you noticed that the last decade has just passed at lightning speed? What significant change did that make in your life to stay satisfied? Asking these essential questions is worth more than all your current assets combined!

What Can This Book Give You?

I wish that each of us should live over a century in good health. But if you found yourself on your deathbed, what thoughts would flood your mind when you think about your life achievements? Do you consider your proficiency in acquiring wealth, land, and gold? It's highly improbable, right?

But most of the average human life ends with many regrets, and their dreams revolve around the graveyard. It is like, "I had lots of dreams but could not get time to implement them." In addition, "I should have lived this way, I should have made clear and early decisions to become a better version, etc." Many people never reflect on their lives until they reach a boiling point.

People often fail to act proactively until disruptions occur, as external factors tend to drive actions more than internal motivations. What stops you from answering the internal call without waiting till boiling point? Is it ignorance? or does our daily routine keep us so busy that we often neglect to respond and act?

"Material possessions will not accompany you when you depart." Nothing comes with you in reality! You must leave everything behind here, no other choice given! After you leave, someone else will immediately inherit all the wealth you've accumulated in your lifetime immediately.

Be aware of a bitter but truth: No one will remember your existence after a few generations. Do you know the names of your great-great-grandfather or great-great-grandmother? You probably never even thought to ask your parents or grandparents. Unless they made a significant impact beyond their own lives, their existence fades from memory—and the same applies to us.

Your legacy, pride, and the positive impact of your actions will act as seeds, ensuring a lasting and meaningful impact for future generations. With this key, one can unlock the doors to receive love, respect, and the ability to leave an enduring imprint on the hearts of others through the intangible values that are carefully cultivated.

What do you gain from this book?

It helps to
- **Know that what belief stops you from identify your winning path**
- **Know your purpose.**
- **Improve your relationships with people to lead a balanced life.**
- **Build your dominant personality and create a brand as a role model.**
- **Develop your self-esteem.**

- **Learn 10 essential techniques to identify your niche and passion.**
- **Uplift your respect and acknowledgment.**
- **Build your confidence to re-start your "real life," irrespective of any setbacks, challenges, or past failures**
- **14 simple approaches to prepare for winning mindset.**

This book is a pathfinder in learning and implementing strategies for every growth-oriented individual who wants to discover their success story and lead a life that leaves a legacy filled with inner harmony.

This book prevents you from having many regrets that would arise at a later stage of your life and helps to kick start in discovering your true potential and start living joyfully in every moment from now.

People have some misconception that joy is always external and conditional, like "I am happy once I achieve this, I am so glad after getting some material things." No, this formula works in other way around.

True joy comes from executing your passionate task with excellence in every hour, minute, and moment.

The sense of "I lived" comes out from your creation or achievements, like an artist.

An artist pours their blood and sweat into their painting journey. During this process, they are entirely absorbed in creating a masterpiece from the depths of their heart, forgetting everything else. They live in every moment of their work. When they finally complete it, they look at their creation with pride.

Nothing can match the joy and satisfaction of experiencing genuine inner fulfillment. This passionate work often leads to outstanding success. However, success, achievements, reaching targets, promotions, or business wins are merely side effects of this passion. Yes, they are just side effects!

Success and failure come and go; they are never permanent. However, the thrilling journey you experienced will remain in your memory forever.

"Engaging in what you are passionate about is the most natural way to live, bringing absolute joy in every moment "

This deep involvement will indeed pay off with more and more success and joy than you imagine. My mentor once said that:

"If you choose elementary tasks every time, you will always work hard. But if you make hard choices, your life will be easy!"

All successful people make tough choices. Notice how successful people's few words become the day's topic? How can they make such an impact with a brief message? Each successful person has made tough choices and poured their heart and soul into working relentlessly towards challenging objectives. So, it is worth increasing the value than volume by making hard choices for a majestic life.

But how can a tough choice make you happy? There's a strong correlation between tough choices and passion. When you make a difficult choice in an area, you're passionate about, it no longer feels tough. Instead, you find joy in every step of the journey, because your passion transforms the challenge into a fulfilling experience.

I am eager to see your success story, and hence, instead of just explaining the techniques, I have mentioned a few practical exercises throughout this book. Have a handy notebook and pen or a device for capturing exercises comfortably. Alternatively, you can mark down the activity listed on the respective page, complete your readings (the entire book) and take down the marked activities and execute them one by one later.

Before continuing, I require two simple but important commitments from you:

Approach this book with an open mind. An open mind helps to receive the messages clearly. "Half a job is already done" when you receive a message with mindfulness. A well-received message will effectively engage the target's imagination. My first requirement is that you approach this book with an open mind, willing to consider different perspectives.

The second one is "Trusting self". What level of trust you should have with you? Let me explain it with a short story. People in a small village gathered to pray for rain. On the day of prayer, only one little boy came with an umbrella! This is trust! So, I wanted to keep tremendous trust in you. "Do you have trust in yourself? Then you have everything and can shake this world!" So, trust yourself until you achieve your dream of the next version!

So, welcome onboard to "Discover Your Dream Next Version" with openness like a child's mindset and unshakable trust in you**!**

Chapter1: Introduction: Key Takeaways

Winning: It brings excitement, confidence, and success, but it also introduces the fear of maintaining that success. People are captivated by success stories because they associate winning with self-esteem, happiness, and security. However, winning is not a permanent state; it is a journey that requires preparation and mental conditioning. Like navigating a new city, success becomes easier with practice and familiarity, but it starts with building the right mindset.

The foundation of consistent winning: It lies in a strong, adaptable mindset. Each challenge should be approached with the intensity of a first timer, always prepared and innovating.

Success is not solely about skill but consistency and breaking through mental barriers. Understanding the purpose behind your drive to win is essential. This book will guide you on how to develop practical strategies, manage expectations, and cultivate a winning mindset to achieve lasting success in life and beyond.

Break old belief to crack your new success: A man passing an elephant camp saw adult elephants tied to small trees with thin ropes. Wondering why they didn't break free, he asked the trainer, who explained that they tie young elephants with these ropes and condition them to believe they can't break them as they grow.
This story teaches us about the power of the mind; if we believe we're limited, we won't attempt to break free, even when we have the strength to do so.

You have full power to take a decision now: Your current state reflects the choices that brought you here, where many settle into a monotonous routine, unaware of the trap. Fortunately, you've made a wake-up call, seizing the chance to find purpose and fulfillment.

Let's explore the vibrant spectrum of life together, filled with growth, excitement, satisfaction, and success. Craft your own story, embracing joy and fulfillment to live an extraordinary life beyond boundaries.

Just pause from routine and reflect now: The daily grind encompasses a structured routine of responsibilities, leaving little room for introspection. Prioritizing the needs of others often takes precedence, leading to a cycle of monotony.

However, it's crucial to pause and reflect, asking probing questions to uncover deeper meaning and purpose. Embracing self-discovery and personal growth amidst the chaos can lead to a fulfilling and transformative journey toward fulfillment and financial independence.

Realize you live in emptiness: In the reality of life, minor victories like promotions or business successes provide fleeting satisfaction, leading to a constant cycle of seeking temporary fulfillment. This pattern, known as the "emptiness cycle," leaves little room for sustained joy and satisfaction, with 80% of your time spent in this state. Despite the rapid passage of time, few PAUSE to reflect or plan for lasting satisfaction, prioritizing external achievements over inner fulfillment.

It's essential to ask listed deeper questions about our purpose and achievements, beyond material success, to find true happiness and satisfaction in life.

Preventing you from regrets: This book offers a comprehensive guide to personal growth and development, focusing on various aspects such as purpose identification, overcoming limiting beliefs, enhancing relationships, building self-esteem for a successful grand life with abundant of wealth.

Chapter 2: The Catalyst to Kickstart Your Transformation

****

"Prioritize information and intelligence, and the money will follow."

-S.M. Watson

Stop, Think Deeply, Reprioritize, Replan and Repositioning yourself

You have been given the precious gift of living a human life. With it comes the unique ability to learn, think, act, and continually improve, building intelligence along the way. As S.M. Watson emphasized in the earlier quote, information and intelligence are invaluable assets.

However, recognizing the presence of the right intelligence and information within yourself can be challenging. Now is the time to step back, view your life from an outside perspective, and reflect boldly.

Let me challenge you to reflect on the following situation. **The game is to imagine that you have only three more years of life span from today**. Now, you have very limited time. So, feel the urgency and write very honest answers to the following questions:

- If I keep going with the same style of this life, where will I end up in this short time?
- If my current path isn't leading to significant change in my life, what adjustments should I make to my daily routine immediately?
- What do I want my lasting image to be in people's minds when they remember me?
- How many people will talk to me if I do not have my current position, business or money? (So, what is my real value?)
- What is holding me back from moving to the next big step and how do I solve it now?
- How do I re-prioritize or remove or delegate or automate my everyday commitments?
- What consistent baby step (actions) should I take to build the right skills, boost my self-esteem, and prepare for bigger steps in my personal development?
- Which circle of people am I currently trying to satisfy? Is it worth the effort, and what changes should I consider?
- What is holding me back from connecting with uplifting growth networks?

- What topic should I strictly defocus on immediately?
- Why don't I consider making a larger impact in the area I'm passionate about?
- What risks am I most afraid to take, and why?
- What actions should I take to overcome this fear by converting open risk to calculated risk?

Finding answers to the above introspective questions will help you break free from routine addiction. This is the first step in discovering your true purpose and understanding what you really want to be known for.

A funny short story about risk taking: A car mechanic, feeling unappreciated, sadly said to an old man, "I'm not paid or respected like doctors, even though we do the same job. I repair all car parts, from the engine to the body, just as doctors do with the heart and all body parts." The old man calmly responded, "Try performing the same operation while the engine is running!

Like a doctor preparing to perform a life-saving operation, ready yourself to embark on the 'operation' of chasing your dreams. This means taking risks, trying new things, and working towards your ultimate goals while also caring for your family. Imagine if all doctors avoided the risk of conducting heart surgeries—patients would face grave danger. Doctors must take these risks to save lives. Similarly, you need to take calculated risks and make smart decisions to achieve your dreams.

We often believe we have plenty of time in our lifespan, but time passes at lightning speed. So, recognize the urgency. Reflect deeply and write honest answers to the above questions. These answers will give you a better understanding of where you are now, serving as a first step. They will provide initial clarity on what you need to focus on—or de-prioritize—to build a meaningful life.

Time, much like currency, is both valuable and limited. Each day, everyone receives an equal deposit of 24 hours. You can choose to spend it or invest it. Investing your time wisely will pay off. The choice is yours!

Time continuously moves forward and cannot be reversed. We often fail to recognize its true value until it's too late. It's important to appreciate each day because once time is gone, we cannot get it back. You might dream of living a remarkable life when you see influential personalities and their achievements. They, too, have the same 24 hours in a day.

Are you waiting for the perfect time? Here's something crucial to understand: many unfulfilled dreams are buried in cemeteries. Their owners were waiting for the 'right time' that never came. I can't let that happen to you. Great achievers are those who take immediate action and never wait for ideal moments or opportunities. They are mindful of their schedules and invest their time wisely in taking meaningful action.

Let's start by reviewing your schedule mindfully. Reflect on how your week went and how you spent each day. Were you happy and satisfied with how you managed your time? If not, can you think what is going wrong and where do you lose your time?

Here's a small task for you: keep your current routine unchanged and approach this exercise with ease and honesty. Each night before bed, set an alarm to record your daily activities from morning until bedtime. Exclude the time spent on basic routines (like bathing, sleeping, getting ready for work, traveling, etc.,). Day by day, record each activity and the time spent on it under two headings: 'Activity Name' and 'Time Spent.' Continue this for the next 10 days.

On the 11th day, review your notes and sum up the hours spent on all activities for each day. Write down this total for each day. Then, sum all these daily totals and label it as 'Tot_Avil_Hrs'."

Ok, now, let's simply classify these activities into two categories: "Spent" or "Invested."

Investment means you spend time for your future personal growth for next decade which is outside your routine, like learning new technical things or reading self-help books, trying to establish new networks for future growth, attending seminars on an entirely new topic, learning any new online courses, attending any mentorship program, creating new ideas, building some new products of your own to hit the market, research on a specific passionate topic, taking training for public speaking, you are in the driver seat in forming a community for a good cause, etc., are some examples.

Underline all these identified as "invested". The rest of the activities comes under are spent category. like watching reels in mobile, office work etc.,

Now, sum underlined (Invested) activities for all days. Call this total as *"Tot_Inv_Hrs"*

Now let's do a little math,

Percentage (%) of your investment = (*Tot_Inv_Hrs / Tot_Avil_Hrs*) x 100

Calculate the above percentage and divide it by 10. Now you will get an average percentage of time invested for the past 10 days.

If the result is greater than or equal to 20%, prepare yourself for noticeable positive changes within a year or sooner. If not, consider ways to reduce time spent on less productive activities and increase time invested in more meaningful pursuits
This exercise will help you understand your strengths and identify areas for improvement in your

investment strategy. The more you increase your time investment, the greater your long-term gains!

This activity may seem simple, dull, or uninteresting, and our brains often trick us into thinking, 'I know everything' or 'I don't need to write it down.' Avoid falling into this mindset. Perform this exercise consciously every day. What seems easy now can become challenging if postponed. If you wait until the end of the week, you might miss out on remembering many activities, leading to inaccurate data. This is how you lose yourself every day.

Often, we miss out on significant opportunities by **neglecting simple, small activities** performed regularly. For instance, we know that dedicating just a little time each day to exercise improves our health, yet we often skip it until health issues force us to spend more time and money on medical care. Similarly, we understand that regularly saving small amounts of money is beneficial for year-end celebrations or vacations, but we ignore it and end up struggling later.

Consistent tiny action holds great power. We don't follow since we don't have patients. Because we require fast results. So, we ignore acting on it, and life gets into stagnate mode. **Tiny actions are better than not taking any action.**

Please understand, this is your ONE LIFE AS HUMAN and ONLY ONE CHANCE. YOU ARE BORN TO BE SUCCESSFUL AND FEEL

FULFILLED and **LEAD A HAPPY LIFE** and **CHARM BY SURROUNDINGS.** Let's **NOT** miss out since there is **NO SECOND CHANCE!**

Get to Know Your Real Personal Power

Do you really want to understand the extent of your power? Let's explore the power of your natural capabilities by examining two different scenarios.

In the first scenario, you've been selected to represent your country in an Olympic running race after a rigorous selection process. You've invested significant effort in training and preparation, including using the right shoes and practicing on quality tracks. It's a tremendous responsibility and a source of national pride to put forth your best effort to achieve your goal for your country.

Everything is set, and you take your position on the track, ready to start your sprint. As soon as you hear the sound of the starting (loud) gun, you launch yourself with all your energy, making your maximum effort to reach the finish line and outpace the competition.

"In the second scenario, you enjoy going on adventures in dense forests and have the chance to explore with a group of like-minded. After walking for a couple of hours, you pause to take photographs of the natural beauty around you, as you love photography. However, while you're focused on capturing images, your team moves ahead, and you end up separated from them. Now, unsure of which direction to take, you find yourself lost in the dense forest.

Now, you spot something moving in the middle of a high-rise meadow about 300 meters away and realize it's a majestic lion. The lion suddenly stops, turns towards you, and stares intently. You know that it sees you as its next meal. What would you do? Without a second thought, you would start running with all your might! The forest floor is uneven, and you're not wearing sportswear, but you would sprint with every ounce of your power, driven solely by the need to save your life. Nothing compares to the intensity and speed of your escape.

Where does this power come from suddenly? Is it borrowed from the outside? No, it's already within you.

Now, let's compare both scenarios:

- The first run is for gold, the second is for survival

- In the first scenario, you're competing with others, pushing yourself to outpace your co-runners and exerting slightly more power than them. In the second scenario, **you're not comparing yourself to anyone; you're running with your maximum potential**, solely focused on survival with no other thoughts.

When we struggle to perform or achieve, we often come up with many excuses for our failure. However, it's crucial to be honest with ourselves. Let me share an interesting short story about Jim Thorpe, who won two gold medals despite facing an unexpected situation just before his Olympic competition.

Jim Thorpe grew up facing significant adversity in his childhood. As a Native American in the early 1900s, he encountered racial prejudice and had a challenging upbringing. His twin brother died at the age of 9, and both his mother and father passed away shortly after, leaving him an orphan. Despite these hardships, he persevered, developed his athletic abilities, and went on to compete in the Olympics.

Just before Jim Thorpe's Olympic competition, someone stole his shoes. Instead of letting it derail him, he found two mismatched shoes that had been discarded in a trash can. To even them out, he had to wear extra socks on one foot. Despite this setback, he adapted and continued with his competition."

Jim Thorpe's story illustrates that nothing can stop you from achieving your goals, if you are determined. When you're running to save your life, you tap into your fullest hidden potential and find no excuses.

Borrow the mindset from the second scenario and apply it to the first. This approach will make you unbeatable. By envisioning an intense, looming danger and eliminating all limiting beliefs, you'll set the highest standards and focus solely on achieving results.

To harness this power effectively, you may need to recalibrate your belief system. It's unwise to reserve your full potential solely for emergencies, as this may lead you to unconsciously wait for a crisis. Instead, adopt a proactive, high-performance mindset. **Focus on one clear goal and take consistent, small steps toward its achievement.**

Applying this technique in real life may be stressful at the beginning. Remember, there's no gain without pain. However, you will eventually conquer many imaginary dangers—self-doubt, inauthenticity, and unfulfillment. In return, you'll discover lasting peace, happiness, and satisfaction!

A few self-reflective questions to help to identify and maximize your full potential truly:

- What sparks my interest when I'm involved in executing a task?
- Does this spark ignite my creativity and motivation each morning?
- Are these creative ideas translated into actions plan to achieve my dream goal?
- Does this action plan hold priority in my daily schedule?

If you find positive and satisfying answers to the above questions, then you've chosen the perfect topic. It will excite and push you. If not, reconsider switching the topic until you find the right answers.

Brain Suspension Trick and Your Simple Game Plan

Even after discovering the right topic, many still fail to succeed. Would you like to understand why this happens and what measures you should take?

Discovering your ideal target state is the next crucial step. You may have already considered this. Setting an ambitious goal often seems simple and motivating, especially when inspired by the recent success of others.

However, once the journey begins, that initial inspiration and motivation can start to fade. Often, you find yourself back at square one. Why does this happen? Where did the intense interest that existed at the beginning go?

It's important to understand this clearly: after the initial burst of motivation, you tend to revert to your original mindset. You are currently in the transition process.

During this transition, as you face challenges, your mind naturally seeks to keep you safe and at peace. It offers safe-zone answers, avoiding risks that could push you out of your comfort zone—sometimes to the point of paralyzing your progress. Understand that this is completely normal. The root cause lies in the following:

When a challenge arises, the boundaries of our current belief system limit your ability to take that risk. Since you're navigating a path, you've never traveled before. Your existing belief system doesn't know how to handle it. Instinctively, it tries to keep you in a safe zone, which is a normal reaction.

"We question every belief except for the ones deeply rooted as our current version."

You've already created a clear mental map of what you believe is possible and impossible. It is shaped by a deeply rooted belief system formed through your experiences. The real challenge begins when you start questioning these foundational beliefs. Confronting and challenging these core beliefs is a risky endeavor for the mind. When you take this risk, your mind's alarm system activates, pulling you back into the comfort zone and returning you to your default way of living. So, how do you address this?

Brain exercise is similar to starting a workout at the gym. Your muscles might ache for a few days as they build strength, but eventually, you'll feel motivated to stay fit. Likewise, by consistently challenging your deeply rooted beliefs and engaging in new experiences through taking on new tasks, your brain gradually adapts, forming new neural pathways to adjust to this new normal.

Additional tips and techniques are explained in more detail in "The Brain Exercises to Break the Pattern and Create New Neural Pathways" (see Chapter 5).

Precious Assets

The human brain is an incredible gift, much like a computer. You can install or reinstall software and upgrade to a new version multiple times, unlearning old techniques and learning new ones to build a fresh mindset. There is one basic requirement: you must trust yourself to achieve what you aspire.

If you start today, you can acquire expert knowledge in any topic within a year, significantly boosting your confidence by this time next year. Consider following powerful quote that resonates with this idea

"All that we are is the result of what we have thought. The mind is everything. What we think we become."

-Gautama Buddha

The most remarkable yet underutilized feature of your brain is its capacity for thinking. Investing time in developing your thinking skills can greatly enrich both your heart and your bank account.

As mentioned earlier, we live in an age where a wealth of information, data, and guidance is available at our fingertips. The challenge is how to efficiently structure yourself to extract the maximum value from this vast sea of information. Some fear that these drastic changes will lead to our demise, a common concern among conservatives during technological revolutions.

However, change is inevitable and will continue regardless of these fears. Remember, those who initially resist will eventually adapt to the new normal, as survival is key!

So, you have precious resources in life such as Time, Thinking and Learning ability. If you use these assets effectively, just get ready to experience great magic in your life!

Taken for Granted and Innocence

One thing to note carefully is that when information was not easily accessible, life was difficult. Now that it's available in abundance, we often take it for granted. The noise of excess information can paralyze our thought process, causing us to lose our sense of self. We struggle to discern what is worth consuming and what is not.

I asked a friend a simple question while he was scrolling on his phone for over an hour in social media: "Can you tell me one thing you learned from the past hour online?" He stared at me, unsure of what to say. This highlights a common issue—we consume a lot of information, but much of it is unrelated, like trying to listen to ten different songs at once. Nothing truly sinks in. In the end, that time spent amounts to nothing done.

This small negligence can lead to significant losses in the long run. It's crucial not to waste any minute, hour, or day. Understand your self-worth and time because your innocence can be someone else's money-making game plan. This world is a mix of good and evil. Without your consent, it exploits your innocence and steals your time, turning you into a consumer. Watching unnecessary content makes you a media-controlled consumer.

I am not against social media. They are doing well in their own space. The problem lies with us. **You watch everything and anything that comes across instead of channelizing what you want to watch.** This habit is like a ship leaving the harbor without a destination.

You are responsible for your life and must take full control of it. With organized focus, you can harness the surrounding resources, enrich your intelligence towards your dream goal. This means, while it's important to avoid getting lost in unwanted content on social media, make a conscious effort to seek out valuable information from it.

"DREAMING HIGH IS NOT A SIN."

~ Indian cricket captain MS Dhoni

Dreaming big as you envision your next version is not a sin. Imagine that you've achieved your dream state—

you'll feel happy and fulfilled, with a strong sense of self. You'll receive care, feel confident, and embrace your authenticity.

Remember, honor is not something you beg for or fight for; it is something others will naturally give you when they feel proud to be in your presence. So, where do you stand? Ask yourself this simple question: without my money, status, or position, how would others treat me? Take a moment each day to reflect on this. Start with small actions and make steady progress toward creating value rather than just focusing on financial gain.

Contribution Requirement at Initial Phase

Discovering your next version is an invitation to discover your purpose, discover the meaning of success, and discover to live a fulfilling life each day. The purpose of discovering your next version is not a destination, but it is a journey to be enjoyed throughout your life.

However, you don't have to fully abandon your current responsibilities to engage in this activity. It needs to start with the 80/20 rule. You give 80% to continue with your regular commitment and find consistent 20% of effort daily to start with. You will gain clarity about managing it through your involvement later.

Imagination of The Best Version

"No matter who you are, no matter what you did, no matter where you've come from, you can always change, become a better version of yourself"

— Madonna

Once, a businessman was in a deep financial crisis, surrounded by demanding creditors and suppliers. Desperate for a solution to save his sinking company, he sat in a park, contemplating his predicament.

Suddenly, an older man appeared before him, sensing the businessman's distress. Upon hearing his problems, the elderly man confidently stated, "I can understand and help your genuine problem since I had also encountered such a situation in the past." In a surprising turn of events, he wrote a cheque for $500,000, signed by none other than Warren Buffet, one of the world's wealthiest individuals.

The businessman, holding the potential solution to his problems, could erase his worries instantly. However, he chose a different path. Instead of cashing the cheque right away, he placed it in his safe, viewing it as a source of strength to rebuild his business, to be used only in terrible emergencies.

The businessman renegotiated deals with newfound determination, restructured his business, and pursued new opportunities. In a few months, he turned his company around, demonstrating that success and fulfillment depended on how he could use his resources.

He returned to the park with the uncashed cheque. As agreed, the old man appeared. However, before the businessman could return the cheque and share his success story, a nurse rushed in and grabbed the old man. I'm so glad I caught him, she exclaimed. I hope he hasn't been bothering you. He always escapes from the mental hospital and tells people he is Warren Buffet. With that, she swiftly took the old man away.

The businessman stood there, stunned. Throughout the year, he believed he had half a million dollars behind him, but it wasn't real. It is an imagined money that turned his life around. His newfound self-confidence empowered him to achieve anything and everything he wanted.

This story is for everyone, regardless of profession, knowledge, or status. If you believe in yourself, you can accomplish amazing things and build outstanding qualities like anyone else.

o------o

Chapter 2: The Catalyst to Kickstart Your Transformation: Key Takeaways

Ask a few mindful questions to understand yourself. This chapter encourages deep reflection on life's purpose and priorities, urging to consider aspirations and seize opportunities. Through the listed thought-provoking questions, it emphasizes the value of taking risks and pursuing dreams. Break free from routine and invest in personal growth and fulfilment, shaping a more meaningful future through introspection and action.

Discover your inner strength and overcome doubts. Here is a story that explains two different running scenarios. In the first scenario, a man runs to win a match for his country. In the second, he runs to survive a dangerous encounter in a forest.

The effort required for the second scenario is unmatched because he is running to save his life, not for a medal. It's the same person, but the second situation demands an unparalleled level of energy, which is already within you. What stops you from using this power in the first scenario?

Jim Thorpe's story also teaches us that challenges can't stop us if we tap into our full potential. By approaching your passionate, positive goals with the same focus and energy as if it were a life-or-death situation, you can achieve incredible things. Try to simulate this mindset to unleash your full energy, give your best, and become unstoppable!

The brain does not allow us to take any risks and tricks to overcome. Based on the experience, the brain builds a belief system over the years.

Whenever you try to break the belief system, that means taking some risk to gain some improvement. Our brain finds it very uncomfortable since survival is the topmost priority.

So, it will constantly try to pull back to the safe zone. This is the core reason to continue the default life than moving to dream life. One should understand and need to break with very small risk-taking tasks consistently to train the brain to build new mental muscles by taking small multiple risk in daily routine like taking unknown route than regular one.

Imagine, you can: Our brains, like adaptable software, thrive on self-trust and dedication to learning. Gautama Buddha's wisdom underscores the transformative power of thought. Efficiently navigating today's information age is key amidst fear of change. Leveraging time and learning yields life's greatest wonders.

Excess and easy information is dangerous: When things become readily available, we often take them for granted, losing sight of their value. In addition to this, the overwhelming noise of information can cloud our judgment and distract us from our true selves. Consuming endless content without direction leaves us empty-handed, akin to listening to multiple songs at once. Our innocence and daily negligence can lead to significant long-term losses.

Effort required to build your next version: This is an ongoing journey towards purpose and fulfillment, not just a destination. Start with the

80/20 rule: allocate 80% to current responsibilities and invest 20% daily towards personal growth, gaining clarity as you progress.

Be proud of the gifts you already have: If I relate this here to this businessperson's story, we always think about what we don't have and feel low. You have already given many gift cheques, such as "your body, your soul, your breath, your imagination, your freedom, learning ability, your health, your parents, your friends and so on and on."

Realize all the priceless gifts already given to you. Move forward with confidence to identify what difference you can make using all these resources as part of discovering your next version.

Chapter 3: Barrier Stones to Self-Discovery: Unlocking the New You

****

"Your time is limited; don't waste it living someone else's life."

-Steve Jobs

Often, you tend to believe that you are the one holding back your well-being and growth. You might think you are the root cause of your procrastination. Instead of acknowledging the various unseen factors that influence your current situation, you constantly blame your fate and shortcomings. What are those unknown aspects that have been skillfully sugar-coated to make you feel down and believe you are at fault? Let me unlock a few secrets here.

Limiting Belief

Long ago, in China, there lived a businessman whose business was to sell combs. Now that he was becoming old and about to retire, he wanted to place the business into wise and able hands.

So, he called forth his three sons and instructed them that their assignment was to sell combs in the Buddhist monastery. The sons were shocked and confused because the monastery monks were bald and never grew any hair. Anyhow, the three sons went about the job that was assigned to them.

After two days, the first son reported he had sold two combs. When the father asked how, he replied he had instructed the monks that the comb would be a valuable tool for scratching their backs in case of itching.

The second son appeared later and said that he had sold ten combs by advising the monks that the combs would help their visitors and pilgrims comb their hair before entering the monastery, as their hair might have ruffled during the journey.

Then the third son came out with a surprising sales figure of a thousand Combs. The father, filled with happiness and anxiety, asked him how he had achieved such a feat.

The third son replied he had given the monks an idea. His idea was to print/emboss Buddha's teachings on combs and gift them to visitors and pilgrims. This would help them remember his teachings while combing their hair daily.

This creative idea struck the deal. The simple story shared by Parikshit Jobanputra [10] leaves a few important lessons for us to learn.

- **It breaks the first limiting belief that people cannot sell combs to monks!**

- **Align your goal so that your stakeholders get more benefits than you.**

- **Motivation lies in creating value on a scale with a compassionate mindset, resulting in an automatic sales volume increase.**

- **Analyze deeply from different perspectives to identify who your ultimate end customers could be.**

- **"Where there is determination, there is always a solution!"**

When a businessman asks his three sons to target selling combs to monks, it may seem like a mad idea due to limiting beliefs. Similarly, it's natural for everyone to have such limiting beliefs and self-doubts.

Let me explain some of the limiting beliefs as explained by team Asana [11] that people carry:

> I am too old to try new things.
>
> I am too young to try new things.
>
> I do not have enough time.
>
> I am not smart enough.
>
> I don't have enough experience for this big career move.
>
> I'll never be successful.

I don't have enough money.

I'll never be one of the best.

I'm not talented enough.

I'll never be an outstanding leader.

Exponential career growth is not possible.

Exponential growth is not possible, particularly in my type of business.

For professionals, a common limiting belief is that career growth must always be linear and time-bound, with exponential growth seen as unnatural or unattainable. This belief arises naturally from observing that most others follow a linear path. Consequently, you might unconsciously adopt this mindset, which can hinder your potential for exponential growth. In contrast, those who challenge this pattern often experience faster and more substantial progress.

Have you not noticed some young people playing top roles as VP/CEO/CTO? Have you not noticed many youngsters have become millionaires in today's world? How is this made possible?

They have tried to alter their internal belief system. It depends on your current determination and belief system. I have seen many companies providing multiple platforms where employees can develop an idea, get funding, and execute it like a CEO until it reaches the market and succeeds. So, being an employee, you can play the CEO's role with your own idea.

What often prevents you from changing your belief system easily is a lack of knowledge or skills. With the right skills, you'll build confidence. It's about bridging the gap: start learning, take small risks by applying these skills consistently to gain real-world experience, and connect with a community of like-minded individuals. This approach will help you uncover the secrets to advancing up the corporate ladder more effectively.

I recall sharing a simple idea with a friend who owns a business. He is an expert reseller of a specific product and is always focused on increasing sales by acquiring more customers. Each month, his goal was to add a few more customers, maintaining this target consistently in mind

One day, I suggested to him, "Since you already have a solid customer base, why not take a step back and think differently? Instead of focusing solely on increasing your customer base, consider gaining knowledge from experts about other products that your existing customers might need. By offering these new products to your current customers, you can effectively double your sales potential with no need to acquire new customers. Any additional customers you gain will be a bonus.

This simple shift in perspective led him to explore new skills and resulted in a remarkable increase in revenue. Since then, adding new products into his portfolio has become one of his primary strategies, complementing his efforts to acquire new customers.

In this context, he believed in continuing the business traditionally, as taught by his ancestors. He firmly believed in running the business in the same old pattern, followed by others. You might also be living with the same mindset, following someone else's path. But remember, you are unique, and you can think differently.

If you observe closely, you'll see that people from the current generation are often unafraid and unashamed to share their thoughts freely on social media, including in video formats. In contrast, those from previous generations might hesitate to appear on social media or embrace the latest technology.

Why this gap? Some grew up in quieter, more traditional environments similar to their parents, while others fear new technology, believing it might limit their thinking abilities, such as with AI.

Here's a secret: this fear is largely unnoticed by the younger crowd. They aren't concerned about others' judgments and treat new trends and technology as a "natural part of life". Their lack of fear allows them to contribute with an open mindset, much like the curiosity and openness seen in children.

Why Don't We Question Our Current Belief System?

Now, let's find out the secret to breaking the limiting belief. We question every belief except our own internal, core beliefs. The essence of your core belief is already deeply embedded in your mind, which is your present version.

Have you dared to question and validate your beliefs? Why is it difficult for you to achieve the status of a CEO or become a multi-millionaire? What is preventing you? Over many years, we have developed strong restrictive beliefs that hold us back.

We remain stuck for years, unaware of this secret. Do you know when your true potential comes out naturally? It happens when you face a profound challenge or loss. Most of our lives are spent on repetitive operational activities. This habit forms our character, which becomes our current version. The sad part is, we do not realize that our best version is sleeping inside!

In his book *Think Outside the Box*, Mr. Som Bathla explains the importance of relearning. Do you remember cassettes or CDs from the past? You could record any song and play it, and you could also rewrite or re-record by removing previously recorded songs.

Similarly, after you were born, you are unaware of any religion, beliefs, or culture, like a blank CD. When you grow up, you record the beliefs shared by your parents, friends, and society. So, now your brain will only sing the song that others have recorded.

Can you ask a question? Why should recording only happen through accidental experiences you gain over life? Why not selectively rewrite a new "song" that helps you achieve your goals and ambitions?

This book, "***WIN INSIDE TO WIN OUTSIDE***," is a life guide that enables you to **THINK, QUESTION, DISCOVER, TRANSFORM**, and most importantly, **CREATE** and **SHARE** values to other lives fully since it is your fundamental right and privilege to live a happy and fulfilling life in this birth!

How does our belief system work? If you believe that becoming your next best version is possible, it becomes true! Conversely, if you view it as an unnecessary effort, risk and believe that a harmonious and fulfilling life is unattainable, that will also be true. Our belief system operates precisely according to our beliefs. So, **BELIEF IS EVERYTHING!**

Trust me, I've been thinking about writing this book for the last decade and have tried many times, but my doubtful mindset held me back. I often lost patience and felt it was impossible. However, reading influential books on belief systems and seeking mentorship advice completely changed my perspective. Once I shifted my belief system, the magic began—help and support started coming to me in various forms.

If you are open enough to understand this shift, the universe will provide all the help to develop your skills. So, I want to ask you one thing, when are you going to kick-start your dream project and hit this world?

No matter what, let's jump in to experience your full potential before you leave this world, irrespective of your current age, gender, environmental conditions, current state, status, and supporting system. You will learn, correct errors, and mature over the years. Once started, you will experience the natural living and satisfaction of your work along with self-acknowledgment!

"Getting rid of a limiting belief means you gotta learn new skills and train for a while."

Periodically take a pause to question your deep-rooted limiting beliefs and then begin anew.

Unconscious Impact of External Forces

External forces are another significant but often overlooked factor that can divert you from your original way of thinking and hinder your natural path to success. What are these external forces?

They include imposed directions, criticism, peer pressure, and societal expectations shaped by your current living environment. These forces begin to influence from childhood, starting with schooling, and continue to Mold into conforming to what society deems necessary for a successful life.

If you are driving a car or bike, you might have experienced something like my experience. Before I start my journey, I pledge to stay calm despite others' behavior on the road.

However, when the incident is a bit serious and crazy (if someone road hog or mindlessly crosses suddenly in your way), we may bust out of our control unknowingly and that feeling ruin for several hours or even sometime mess up that day.

Similar to this scenario, in this race of living, when external impact is strong and repeated, you lose yourselves.

Imagine someone you know has just received a spectacular offer or promotion. You might think, "How am I any less than that person? I deserve something better, too." This list of pressures keeps growing. You don't feel jealous, but **you start doubting your abilities**, questioning why you haven't received similar or even greater recognition.

So, what impact can it create for you?

- When this happens repeatedly, it kills your creativity, innovation, and inner peace.

- If we continue to be there in this state of mind, slowly, this becomes your behavior, and regular behavior turns to habit, habit becomes character or lifestyle, and lifestyle becomes our image; this image is nothing but your version! So, the external world perceived this version. You sculpt your version with every move like this!

Some external impact looks very natural and creates unconscious action by you. For example, when you're driving and someone on a super bike speed past you, revving their engine to show off their speed, sound, and pride, you might instantly feel a dent in your self-worth. Your ego is touched, and you feel the urge to accelerate and chase after them.

So, what's really happening here? What are you losing in this process? While chasing after them might bring temporary satisfaction and excitement, you could end up failing to reach your destination. In the broader sense, you might even lose sight of your own destiny and identity.

Regardless of your preferences, external influences and pressures continually affect you in various ways. Unconsciously, these repeated forces gradually shape a version of you that may not be truly your own. After a while, you may find yourself feeling exhausted and bored. Society often teaches us to imitate or compete with others, pulling us away from living our own lives authentically.

Now, let's focus on how to become your own version. You can't prevent external forces from affecting you, but you can change how you respond. When someone's actions frustrate you, your mind becomes unsettled and demands an immediate reaction. Afterward, you may find yourself apologizing for your behavior, realizing that you might have already lost future opportunities. This could mean you've damaged your image.

Emotions play a significant role in tempting you to react to temporary satisfaction. However, this doesn't mean you should never react. In fact, reacting can be crucial in certain situations, such as emergencies, accidents (like saving someone), escaping from danger, or even in moments of humour.

Emotions need to be managed when someone or something negatively disturbs your mind. The most powerful yet underutilized ability you possess is your "ability to think deeply."

However, unmanaged emotions can paralyze this ability, preventing you from seeing the bigger picture. The burning desire to resolve an issue may confine your mind to a narrow perspective.

In moments of intense emotion, it's crucial to take a break and resist the urge to react immediately. By expanding your perspective and seeking solutions beyond the immediate problem, you gain a more comprehensive understanding of the situation.

Every critical situation carries an underlying intention or agenda that needs to be deeply analyzed, a process known as critical thinking. A permanent solution can often be found by using the "5 Why" method, which involves repeatedly asking "why" to each answer you receive until you uncover the root cause. This method leads to a permanent fix. This shows maturity in handling problems in tough situations.

Maturity means managing current emotions clearly with positive thinking. Taking complete control of yourself at any (emotional) moment, having a deep breath, pausing, looking deeper into the issue or opponent, and analyzing the problem from the opponent's side to understand the impact caused by the situation. This is thinking beyond.

During this pause, aim to respond reasonably without causing harm or seeking revenge. This helps to respond with more analysis and evidence.

If you realize that the current situation created is just a play or hate game (using your critical thinking ability and 5 why method), exhibit your strong value by helping them in a critical moment and leave a smile. This is the world's most powerful punishment one can gift.

However, don't worry much about the past. You cannot alter the past image created. "If one bad chapter doesn't mean your story is over!" You can take full control of your life now to pause, review, re-correct, and re-build your new image. Now, you can be conscious of every act. Let's do the magic of your transformation. Understand and start applying all the values you get from this book.

A Story About Managing Self

A gazelle is a graceful little one, a particular variety of deer or antelope native to Africa and Asia. Gazelles are extremely fast, running up to 60 miles per hour. Lions love to eat gazelle meat. But it's tough for lions to catch gazelles because the latter run so fast.

So, once upon a big grassy plain [6], lions desired to catch gazelle. But as said, catching gazelles was tricky because they could run super-fast. So, instead of running after them, a bunch of young lions devised a clever plan using old lions that could not run faster.

In the game plan, young lions formed a half circle on one side, and old lions formed the same pattern on the opposite side.

The young lions slowly navigate through tall grass very near to the curb of Gazelles and roar at them. This action will guide the gazelles in a particular direction. Thinking they were heading to safety, the gazelles sprinted away from the lions, who couldn't catch up.

Unknown to them, they were being led straight into another lion group. These were older lions who were too tired and worn out to join the chase. They were missing some teeth and weren't as strong as they used to be. But they had a surprise up their sleeves.

As the gazelles approached, the old lions suddenly jumped up and roared louder than the young lions. The scared gazelles, thinking there was a new danger, turned around and ran straight back into the mouth of the young lions.

This tale offers a lesson, life advice of all sorts. It's like said, "Run towards the roar!" The idea is that avoiding problems or fears might seem safe, but it can lead to even more significant issues. Just like the gazelles find themselves in a tricky situation, we might get stuck and unhappy if we run away from our fears.

The lions we fear may not be dangerous in our daily lives, but they often turn out to be false alarms. Constantly running from these fears can result in a life of unhappiness.

It's normal to experience fear in our everyday lives. However, it's essential to understand that courage is not the opposite of fear. One can move forward with fear while still having great confidence is real courage.

Being still and allowing fear to control us is not enough to achieve results. It is important to take reasonable precautions, consistently act despite fear, and continue moving forward. This approach empowers one to navigate life's tall grass path of uncertainty and control their destiny.

Why do people choose a default life over striving for something better? Is it simply due to a fear of failure? While this may be partially true, the larger factor is often a "**fear of success**". People often fear the unknown and challenges that accompany success, which makes them hesitate to pursue bigger goals and ambitions.

Once we reach our target, we often worry about maintaining our success and status. It's similar to running from one problem to another (like running from lions). Instead of constantly running away from the fear of failure or fear of success, view it as a journey, much like the interplay of light and dark in a day. Life truly begins when you are determined to face your fears!

Your Younger Version

Imagine a ten-year-old version of yourself sitting opposite you now. Would you tell this little girl or boy, 'You are an embarrassment,' 'You are worthless,' or 'You are useless'? It would feel unfair to say such things, right?

Realize that this is essentially what you do to yourself daily. Many did not well understand this. You're not just saying these words. If you lack a big life goal, you're merely rehearsing and affirming these statements.

What would you say to this child? You'd likely tell them they are amazing and should ignore any negative opinions, right?

Let me tell you this: You are incredible! You are valuable! You are amazing! And you can do it! How would you feel if you said this to yourself every day and took conscious, consistent action towards your growth?

Life of Animal

Let's consider the life of an animal. After birth, it learns to hunt for food, sleep, fight for territory, and reproduce. This cycle continues until one day, it dies. It's impossible to train a lion not to eat meat or teach a goat to eat meat; they are hard-wired by nature. However, humans can choose to be vegetarian or non-vegetarian based on their environment and learned behaviors.

As a child, you have few skills beyond crying when you need food. While we may not have any preloaded knowledge, we are born with an innate ability to continuously learn and think, which allows us to shape our lives. This is an incredible freedom. As human beings, we have the unique capacity to be trained and to adopt new skills and perspectives throughout our entire existence!

Leaving this world without achieving anything is like living in a forest with decent clothes. Nature did not choose you for this purpose. Your purpose in being here is not simply to passively enjoy what is provided for you. If you truly love your passion, you can use your gifted thinking power to create your own unique version.

You can share your deep love, effectively communicate your passion, and establish it as a powerful brand, leading to a life filled with love and purpose. Being part of such a fulfilling life generates an incredible amount of positive energy, enabling you to flourish each day. In return for the love you show, you can expect to receive admiration and affection from others. Be the first to take your steps

Getting to know about people's reality

A mother and two little daughters. She decided to give them an apple to enjoy as a snack. She invited them to come and pick one apple each, mentioning that she had left two apples for each person at the breakfast table. The younger sister rushed to the table and quickly bit into the first apple and grabbed the second apple and took a bite before her sister arrived.

When the mother saw this behavior, she was about to tell her younger daughter it was a wrong act and unacceptable.

Meanwhile, the second daughter ran and reached the breakfast table, surprised to see both apples in the younger one's hand. The younger sister peacefully extended one apple to her elder sister and said, "This is very delicious and take it", she had offered the tasty one to her sister.

After observing her child's behavior, the mother realized she had been too quick to judge and was ashamed. She realized that her premature judgment could have hurt her daughter's open-mindedness and optimistic character. We commonly make snap judgments based on a few positive or negative actions and then permanently label people in our minds. No label is permanent!

We often believe our current version is correct, but valuable contributions can come from anyone, even those we considered useless earlier. "We do not have the right to disrespect anyone based on our label mechanism. It is the most inhumane act one can commit."

Maintaining a balanced life, irrespective of your knowledge level or cleverness in front of others, is always better. Your environment offers a unique learning opportunity. What significant assets do we have of our own? Nothing! Everything we have is borrowed from others or the surrounding environment, even our bodies that we receive from our parents!

We can't fully understand someone's life, their upbringing, and the reasons behind their behavior. Be cautious of those who only display goodness in your presence. While doing so, don't underestimate someone because of a few incorrect actions. Strive to grasp **the inner motivation** behind each act and make a fair judgment.

But remember to create your own strong boundary and learn to say, "No", if really required. You can't be available to everyone all the time, nor should you try to fulfill everyone's needs.

There is confusion regarding being nice and pleasing. Being nice is ok, this means being kind to others. But you will never please everyone, leaving your value flying in the air unattended. Even if you treat everyone with respect, consideration, even love, some will not appreciate it. Others will dislike you simply for being so nice to the people they themselves despise. **So, without compromising your values, you can be nice to people.**

In this world, no belief remains constant, and no one is perfect. Everyone appears good until they make a mistake. This doesn't mean they are bad; sometimes, situations lead people to make wrong choices. Instead of judging who is good or bad, move beyond a fixed mindset, since it does not contribute to your growth.

Transform your approach by engaging with others with a positive, open-minded attitude, regardless of any personal benefits. Embrace a childlike mindset, focusing on genuine interactions and personal development.

But to discover your best version, you may have to endure the pain of losing some toxic people around you. These individuals can be dangerous and poisonous, using "appreciation" as their weapon to manipulate you, especially when you're emotionally vulnerable.

Very often, they offer praise even for small actions. You need to learn to identify the difference between genuine support and toxic behavior. The thought of losing them can be uncomfortable, especially if you've grown accustomed to their constant presence—their validation becoming as addictive as a drug. But remember, **the pain of losing toxic people today will only make you feel the power of tomorrow!**

The Journey Towards the Center of a Better Relationship

You run for the family towards building a better life. We work hard to achieve this goal. Remember, we choose a job or business to earn money and live a better life. But mostly in the job or business battle, earning good respect, a promotion, an excellent position, and a good income becomes the central attraction of life.

Your entire life revolves around business or profession. Initially, you might have run for the family, but later, you might have emotionally "run away" from family. In the process, you might overlook the crucial realization that your main purpose is to improve the quality of life for your loved ones. But? Do you feel that you missed out on truly living with them? Stop, turn around, and think about how to bridge the emotional distance you've created.

In a busy schedule, you may forget to express love and gratitude to your loved ones. Their proximity provides us with great comfort and confidence. We do not even remember to tell them they are very important to our success. But we expect other way around. We expect they need to listen to our problems.

Sometimes we misuse our loved ones as outlets for our external emotional struggles, harming them indirectly by taking them for granted. Unfortunately, we often realize this only after we've lost them permanently. It could be your father, mother, spouse, siblings, children, or an uncle. They sought your time and closeness, not your wealth.

If you face relationship challenges with anyone, ask this one question to yourself: How would I behave to them if today was my last day? You will automatically subtle your anger, anxiety, vengeance, politics, tricks, and downplay, won't you?

Managing a good relationship is crucial for mental well-being. It requires constant effort. Managing means expressing your emotions explicitly to them about **"how important they are to you". So, they are not only just near to you, but how close to you!** This creates a positive vibration in your living environment and keeps you motivated and focused on your goal with no distractions.

Celebrating your small wins with them keeps you highly motivated. Maintain good relationships in your personal and professional life. Be the first to appreciate and make someone happy daily. This investment is guaranteed to provide you with a double return. You don't need money to build this, but little time from you!

Most importantly, have at least one person whom you can trust completely, someone with whom you can share every pain and problem (if it's sharable) to manage your mental health throughout your life. This person doesn't need to offer advice or help; just listening is enough. Never expect assistance or support, but make sure this person is truly trustworthy and will never exploit your vulnerability for their own gain, since you may end up creating a cheater. Be aware of what to share and what not.

It's okay if you don't have someone nice to share with. I have explained a 15-minute sitting mental exercise to burn out your pains under the title "Pause to generate energy technique!" in chapter 5. Please follow it and burn out your pains every day to free yourself from worries to become more energetic. It is a very simple but powerful technique.

So, start your hero life by discovering your next best version, which reflects excellent characters, and live like a role model irrespective of external emotional impact! No significant investment is required; just a mind shift and begin your new life, discovering your new version in relationships!

How Do You Keep Self-Motivated When You Are Completely Down?

Ok, let's look at how. List your achievements, even small ones. Write the situation, challenges you faced and overcoming from it any great wins. The idea is to get excited when you read it later. Title this as **"My wonders"**

- Your education related (completed your education with great difficulty or you were outperformed in a particular subject)
- Contest wins (small or big) / received awards /
- You got many promotions.
- Your leadership team appreciated you for your multiple achievements.

- You have opened your own business or tried out something new (failed or success, but there is great learning, and you tried it out!)
- Your new idea worked out.
- You have mentored some people, and they came to you thanked and shared their success stories.
- Compliments from your professional contribution or all business wins / revenue increased.
- Some people are grateful for you, as you've uplifted their lives.
- Your own achievements are what you really feel great about it.
- What materials things that you bought as part of your life ambition (a house or your dream car).
- You made a big impact out of your presentation.
- A new skill learnt and done surprise demo and got appreciated.
- Come across many difficult times and still achieved successfully.
- Birth of your first baby.

- Any professional achievements, like your leadership initiative, transformed your organization or business.
- You had escaped from some dangerous situation, or you saved someone from a similar situation.
- Piece of your artwork or any personal skill, you feel great about yourself.

Your unique character is like you are honest with all, you are a peaceful person or your lovely smile or you are so funny, not betrayed anyone until now, capture all your unique values and achievements.

|| Take a moment to relax and try completing this task. Keep this summary in an easily accessible place and update it regularly as life progresses. Most importantly, refer to it during challenging times to find support and perspective. ||

Respecting yourself with a positive mindset helps you achieve great heights, regardless of the situation. The exercise above helps you quickly recall this and feel good. Most of the time, our brain tends to focus on what we lack, leading to feelings of inadequacy.

This sense of inadequacy can lead to insecurity about trying new things. Maintaining a positive and grateful perspective on your current life boosts your confidence as you move to the next level. Make a list of your blessings and remind yourself of them when you're feeling down to witness your personal growth and achievements. The more you feel proud of yourself, the greater your success in life!

Impact Your Value at Scale with Compassion

What does "impacting at scale" mean? We do some passionate work that benefits our inner self. But it should also help people in need at the same time. In the evaluation of human life, humans were hunting for food. Slowly, they transformed into farming.

Though farming did not give good returns. But they still started farming since it solved not only individuals' hunger but also all-around society. This was providing fulfillment to farmers rather than earning money. So, if we choose to do any task passionately, we can attach a human touch to how we can support those in need around us.

Making a Small Difference to A Few Matters!

A small story to understand the profound, routed, simple concept. On the beach, a man witnesses a girl throwing starfish back into the ocean. He wonders why she bothers, as there are so many starfish. The girl picks up another starfish, throws it into the sea, and says, "I made a difference to that one."

This story teaches us that even small actions matter. Doing even a small act of kindness can create a positive impact.

Some books are eye-openers and create a significant impact on our lives. It will make us rethink building new characters and re-designing new life. My humble message through books aims to save my fellow humans from the worst failures and deep regrets, as I am eager to witness many fulfilling lives.

You can regain money, but what about hope, life, a good relationship, good company, and care? It all comes if you internally feel fulfilled. I am happy even if this book gives one minor change in your life; I made a difference like the above story!

Forgiveness is the Key to Success

We always carry a lot of baggage from past failures, hurt, cheating, etc. Before trying to build your new version, it is very important to clear this baggage from your mind. If, despite your hard work, you find it difficult to envision or make progress toward your goals, it's a sign that you're still carrying the heavy baggage of past failures or rejections.

Take the first step and forgive yourself for not being nice to yourself before. You are focused on caring for others but neglecting yourself. It's time to change this pattern and shift your priorities. Start by considering how well you care for your mental well-being. If you feel stressed, those around you will likely feel the same. Don't dwell excessively on what's already happened. You can't change the past, and worrying about it won't benefit you. Unfortunately, time machines don't exist to undo mistakes. If exists, it will create a record in sales!

Let's decide today: Forgive yourself first and extend that forgiveness to others who have wronged you. To achieve peace, it is necessary to forgive those who have caused the immense pain that lingers in your memory. Otherwise, you are repeatedly hurting yourself countlessly and you cannot focus on your own growth. Forgiveness is difficult but try to do it for your well-being.

Unless you forgive, you cannot move further, since this baggage will always sit at the top of your mind and consume most of your energy. Do not forget the worst that happened in your life since they taught an excellent lesson but try to forgive those who created the situation.

Unknowingly, you could also be an innocent reason for the same. Yes, you have given enough opportunity for others to play with your life. So, learn from this experience and ensure that you do not repeat it, but forgive everyone and move on by taking complete control of your life!

This is the only way to identify your next beautiful version! Now, let's explore selecting the perfect topic for you in the next chapter.

o------o

Chapter 3: Barrier Stones to Self-Discovery: Unlocking the New You: Key Takeaways

Limiting belief is like a mirage, deceiving and elusive. Chinese businessman seeking a successor to sell combs in a Buddhist monastery. Despite the initial skepticism, the third son proposes a creative idea—printing Buddha's teachings on combs.

When people comb every time, they remember this teaching. This innovative approach leads to significant sales. The key takeaways include breaking limiting beliefs, focusing on providing value to stakeholders, emphasizing compassion in mindset over mere sales, and emphasizing that where there is a will, there is a way. The story aims to challenge common limiting beliefs and self-doubts in individuals.

It is important to be brave enough to challenge your own deeply held beliefs. Let's take one sample question: What is preventing you from becoming a vice president of an organization?
If you don't question yourself, your mind will be convinced it's not for you permanently. It all starts with mindful questions. This book serves as a **life guide, empowering you to think, question,**

discover, transform, and, most importantly, create and share values that **allow you to live the life you've always dreamed of.**

Here's a story from my own life. A while back, I shared a simple idea with a well-known business owner that dramatically boosted his sales over a few years. He had been focused on increasing his customer base each month.

I suggested he pause and consider adding a new commodity to his portfolio, leveraging the trust he already had with existing customers. This approach allowed him to double his revenue without needing to find new customers. So, this approach made him come out of traditional business limiting belief. Since then, expanding his product line has become a key strategy for his business.

External forces influence our behavior and shape our identity, often unconsciously. Society's pressures to imitate or compete divert us from our authentic path, leading to temporary satisfaction but long-term disconnection from our true selves.

Emotions play a significant role in our reactions, often limiting our thinking and problem-solving abilities. However, by pausing, analyzing, and responding with maturity, we can transcend temporary fixes and address the root causes of our challenges. Taking control of our responses empowers us to shape our own narrative, leaving behind past images and crafting a new, authentic version of ourselves.

Face the fear. A story about how a group of young lions devised a clever plan to catch gazelles by using the fear of older lions. It teaches to "run towards the roar," facing fears rather than avoiding them. Courage isn't the absence of fear but moving forward despite it. Being afraid of both failing and succeeding leads to a default life. Embracing challenges with courage defines true living.

How are you treating yourself every day? Imagine your younger self sitting opposite to you. It is unfair to tell him about his inability daily. If you **are not taking action to move forward, then understand that you are telling this to you every day** unconsciously. Instead, demonstrate your greatness by taking action towards success.

You're not meant to just settle for the default life. In the animal kingdom, creatures follow instinctual patterns from birth to death. Humans, however, possess the unique ability to learn, think and adapt, shaping their lives according to their desires. Nature didn't intend for us to merely exist.

You have the freedom to create your own purpose and leave a meaningful legacy. By following your passions and utilizing your thinking power, you can craft a fulfilling life filled with love and purpose, earning admiration from others in return.

Don't rush to label people. In a short story, the mother's observation of her daughters' behavior teaches a valuable lesson about snap judgments and the potential for growth in every individual. Rather than labeling people based on limited actions, strive to understand their motivations and nurture open-mindedness. It's crucial to maintain boundaries and prioritize self-respect while treating others with kindness. True growth often requires letting go of toxic influences, even if initially uncomfortable, to pave the way for a brighter future.

Handling self when feeling completely down, it is unnecessary to get any motivation from outside. It lies in you. Create a list of past achievements titled "**My Wonders**" including educational accomplishments, contest wins, business ventures, mentoring successes, professional achievements, personal skills, and unique qualities. Reflecting on these successes instills positivity, fostering confidence to tackle challenges and get your energy back in your control.

"**Impacting at scale**" means making a profound difference in the lives of others through compassionate actions, aligning passionate work with supporting those in need. Your impactful value delivery should **positively influence and uplift**

numerous lives, in addition to your own success strategy.

Can you make a difference to one's life? A girl throwing starfish one by one back into the ocean from the seashore. Surprised by this act, a man questioned, "there are so many on the shore, what it would make a difference." She replied after throwing another one, "I made the difference to the life of that one fish" and she continued. This story emphasizes the importance of kindness and its ability to create positive change, inspiring us to make small differences wherever we can. This will give enormous fulfillment.

Forgiveness is essential for personal growth and success. By letting go of past failures and hurt, you free yourself from the weight of negativity that holds you back. **Start by forgiving yourself and then extend that forgiveness to others**. Holding onto grudges only hinders your progress and consumes your energy. Learn from experiences but choose to forgive and move forward with a renewed focus on your goals.

Chapter 4: Clarity–How to Choose a Topic?

****

"If you keep doing what you've always done, you'll keep getting what you've always gotten."

~ HENRY FORD

10 Ways to Identification of Your Topic

How do you identify your passionate topic? If you rewind some of your experiences from time to time, you may identify an interesting topic and get involved in execution. Initially, you may be happy to see that it was a pleasant topic. After traveling for a few months, however, the initial excitement gradually diminishes, leading to decreased motivation and ultimately abandoning the endeavor. You may have repeated these many times in the past.

Why did this happen? and why did interest decline over time? The reason is simple: we chose these topics based on the influence of the trend or hype in the external environment. If AI becomes prominent in ads and portrays itself attractively, people will aspire to learn or attempt something.

If the topic loses its traction, people lose interest in it, and you also lose focus. We unknowingly lose the time spent. Losing a lot of time starts with this first trap.

Why did this happen, and why did interest decrease over time? The answer is simple: our choice of topics was driven by external trends and hype. When any new arrivals, any topic or product dominates advertisements and is presented in a compelling way, people are drawn to learn about it or try it out. However, when the topic loses its appeal, so does the public's interest, and consequently, focus diminishes. This shift results in a significant loss of time, if it is irrelevant to you. This is the first trap in life.

It's not that you should ignore current changes—embrace them. However, prioritize your time wisely. Focus on what's essential for your survival and concentrate on your primary goals. The world is with full of noises. Do these noises hold true meaning for you? Directing your attention where it truly matters can become your guiding light.

Let's also discuss a few internal noises. We excel in multiple areas and aim to achieve greatness. However, there is no clarity about selecting a topic since mental math about "return on investment" calculation never allows us to choose a topic. you may struggle with decision-making altogether.

On the other side, "starting trouble." Where to start and how to start? You will remain stagnate and regret when others show some achievements in the same field. So, prolonging because of starting trouble holds you back. Life goes on with a busy routine, keeping a thought in one corner of my mind, "I should start sometime." This is the giant second trap. What's the best way to begin? "Just begin it" somewhere. The starting point has no right or wrong. Eventually, you'll adopt the correct approach.

Otherwise, if you choose one topic to focus on, another equally enticing topic will continuously compete for your attention, drawing you away. This distraction means you end up making minimal progress on each topic, merely satisfying your own curiosity. As a result, you risk becoming a "Jack of all trades but master of none." Beware—this is a perilous third trap that wastes time and leads to stagnation. In the end, you may find yourself nowhere.

These chaotic circumstances can cause you to become a victim of procrastination and prevent you from taking decisive action or living with clarity. First, identify this pattern in life, try to break free from this self-trap, tune away from such internal noises, and identify your true "one topic" to focus on at a time.

Let's move on to the core. Focus solely on the upcoming exercise, clearing your mind of any distractions. So, do this activity in your most productive time (preferably early morning after a good sleep, but I leave it to your convenient choice). Choose a peaceful location, free from distractions. Free up your mind from overthinking about implementation challenges now.

Ok, now please take out your trusty pocket notebook and jot down your thoughts using the following exercise:

Take one fresh page and title it "My life dream project." Draw a table with five columns. Title the initial column as "My Passion. Use the below listed scenarios as guidance for your responses in the first column.

1. Have you ever had a scenario where you experienced satisfaction or happiness from a small act of self-fulfillment? You were so excited when you did this activity. Start looking around even for small fulfillments that touch your heart. What was that? Give a deep thought to what you can do for this to impact at scale? If you get more answers, number them and write one after another.

I would like to share a true story [4] to relate to the above context to recall and get similar ideas.

Once upon a time, Dr. Abdul Kalam (former president and called a missile man of India) visited a school to attend a function. He watched some children with disabilities walking slowly with great difficulties using artificial limbs. He read the discomfort on their faces! Out of curiosity, he examined the weight of artificial limbs and discovered the cause of discomfort. Each of them weighed almost 4 kilograms!

Dr. Kalam was concerned about them and returned with the heavy-hearted question, "How can I help these kids?" The next day, he called his former team, shared this problem, and brainstormed about a space-age, lightweight material that his team already used in space crafts. They subsequently created a lightweight artificial limb that weighed 10 times less than the existing one.

It was a magnificent gift for those children to walk easily. "When I see children run around and cycle with the artificial limbs we designed, it is sheer bliss," Kalam shared while delivering a convocation program in 2010. In another interview, he mentioned that this was one of the most fulfilling achievements in his lifetime.

So, fulfilling is something different from your skills and specialization. When your skills, contentment, and societal requirements merge, you emerge as life's champion. Recall such past life experiences and write a heart-touching activity in which you were engaged.

Ok, let's move on to identify more niches using another technique.

2. Close your eyes and let your mind wander back to your childhood, immersing yourself in the memories as you explore and answer these thought-provoking questions. What amazed you as a child? What do you aspire to become during

childhood? Who inspired you during your childhood? Who was your practical life hero? Did you ever think that I should also become like this person? Write all your deep wishes.

While writing, you may observe that some aspirations appear irrelevant at first glance. But let's do a deep analysis and make modern modifications. You can reshape it later.

Short sharing about my personal experience. During my schooling time, I wanted to learn how to draw comic characters using computer graphics because reading many comic books had influenced me. I wanted to give life to these characters (now it is called animation). Now witness the immense growth of this industry! Lots of movies from "Finding Nemo" to today's "Iron Man" what an excellent animation work! This industry grows to the next level in creating any imagination using AI, marching towards massive growth!

Ok. I had this crazy interest but what makes sense now for me to identify this as childhood desire and what can I do with it? Since I am completely into a different field now. However, I can modernize this passion in alignment with my current skill to build something new. I can teach complex math using animation to provide a quick learning experience for kids. So, this is how we can modernize and give life to our burning aspirations. So, every crazy thought which is deep routed as dream can be modernized now. So, do not worry about the quality of your dream idea or project, just bring it to the table now.

The burden of various situations and obligations could have pushed those dreams aside, causing them to fade from your thoughts. It is fine. Forget about regrets. You excelled at adapting to what was necessary for survival during that time. **But you can always restart**! **You have the freedom to restart your life many times until you are alive and healthy**. The only person holding you back from restarting is "You." Grant your soul the liberty to live the life it longs for.

Remembering your childhood memories fills you with immense joy and excitement because they are filled with powerful emotions. You might have aspired to become a pilot, own a flight, create comic books, be a great artist, direct a movie, or work in a prestigious company. Write without analyzing the execution path or evaluating the idea. This is not important now. Important is to capture your passion statement with no predetermined mindset.
Ok, let's move on to the next technique.

3. Think back to that unexpected, profound problem that you never fathomed encountering in your lifetime, yet you bravely faced it head-on. There could be many others suffering from the same

issue across the world. Where are you? Why not build a structured program from your past lessons and share the knowledge with online coaching by getting help from the right mentor? By taking few steps, you have the power to save countless lives.

4. Sudden shocks from someone we trust (anything from losing people, relationship issues or great gain or loss from a partnership). But you have managed it well. You encountered obstacles and developed multiple strategies to overcome them. Do you have such a live experience?

Why don't you teach and share those lessons out of this suffering? You can surely save some lives, which gives excellent fulfillment. You're not the only one facing this problem. Many people might be deeply going through such issues with heavy depression. Formulate and create a system like a training bundle for online coaching. Let the world see your motherliness! So, list down such activities.

5. If someone touches a topic in a conversation, you are excited and will talk about it for hours. It could be a knowledge or hobby. Can you elevate this topic to a higher level? Please deeply consider how to use this knowledge for the betterment of our world.

6. If you have had long-term health issues, you have found a technique to overcome them! Try planning it with the help of a coach, and you can kick-start your service to teach others and save lives.

7. Try to revisit your past years. Recollect all the feedback that you received. Some individuals, whether strangers, your team, or friends, may have acknowledged your proficiency in "one thing". You might do this tirelessly without realizing you are good at it. Do you remember that one thing? Can you write about that topic or skill? Can you work on taking the next level to impact on scale?

8. You are very good at technical topics from your massive experience. You had faced a real-time problem where no books can teach compared to your practical experience. It saves others a lot of time. Could you structure it from basics to advanced program to build your training program?
You don't even need to appear on screen. Lot of AI tools do the job for you. You only need to write or dictate the script. Why don't you explore and serve people waiting to get this help? This deep knowledge with authentic examples definitely impacts at scale!

9. You are very good at leadership, and it is your core skill. Many people suffer and halt their professional progression because of gaps in their emotional, communication, or other skills. They may also not know how to handle corporate tricks, which blocks their progress even if they are good at technical things. Do you have an idea to help at scale?

10. You might think for a very long time to achieve something as your life goal. Give it a shot to write now. Because of time constraints and the environment, you couldn't make any effort. What goal do you have and if it is possible to start with a small action such as learning some deep knowledge about it? (your life goal may be big or small, it doesn't matter such as imagination of ultra-modern farming, owing a big factory, starting an accident-free world initiative, no human begging for food, or a new firm starting etc.,)

I'm sure you generated a long list of ideas from this exercise. Now, let's capture all these ideas what you have got out of the above explained method captured in a table with following captions.

Let's draw a table as shown below with the first column titled as "Passion statement". Let's write down all the captured ideas or your dream passion project here.

Now, in the second column titled as "skill requirement and rating column", write all the skills needed or available to you. One additional activity here is to evaluate these skills based on your current knowledge level as basic, medium, or high.

In the third column, titled as "What can you offer as an individual (to this world)?" out of your passion. Write the relevant information as stated in the column tile.

In the fourth column, write a title, "What burning need can this solve? You may have to do some research here. **Sometimes, it's valuable to create the need when people lack awareness of its importance.**

So, be creative in creating awareness of the need and its benefits if you are passionate about a particular topic. Take a look at the table below to get a better understanding. It has a few examples:

Passion statement	Skill requirement and rating	What can you offer as an individual?	What burning need can this solve? (Score out of 10)	Your passion priority (Score out of 10)

Leadership development	Communication–**High** Presentation –**Medium** Problem-solving - **High**	Coaching	Resolve career blocks. **Score: 8**	6
Singing	Singing voice– **M*edium*** Tone– **Medium** Breath control - **High** Pitch– M**edium** Musicality– **High** Vocal lessons- **A*verage*** Rhythm- **Medium** Diction- M**e*dium*** Audience awareness- **High** Music knowledge– ***Average***	Sing, compose songs, entertain people and teach singing.	See the real happiness in people. Ignite people's joy, love, awful life, meaning and feeling good. Inspirational to self **Score: 6**	7

	Identify and assess the listed entrepreneur skill set (listed sample)			
Want to become a CEO/CTO/VP / Top leader / top businessperson	1. Leadership 2. Communication 3. Networking 4. Strategy 5. Time management 6. Business management 7. Problem solving 8. Listening /Adoptability 9. Sales 10. Creative thinking 11. ...	Profit to the organization Or Serve people with my new product.	Inspirational to self and others Generate more job opportunities. contribute to GDP growth for the nation. **Score:8**	9

Once you've compiled an extensive list of potential interests, the next step is to calculate the scores of the last two columns and add them together. The topic with the highest score shows not only a personal connection but also its relevance and importance in the current world scenario. In case of a tie, prioritize the topic that resonates most deeply with you personally.

How do I know if my chosen topic is right for me now?

Sometimes, our mind biases us based on the situation and our internal hidden agenda. The goal of financial gain drives the domination of solving a pressing problem, automatically forces you to increase the score of the second parameter (passion priority).

Let's understand an important thing here: Identifying the burning need is a must. No compromise, but your passion holds greater significance than any world-altering problem or your problem-solving ability.

Why Do I Say This?
Your "Passion priority" will always be sustained because it strongly connects to your personal emotions like a pure love of your mother or father. You cannot compromise this to decide based on the current burning need and your ability!

Why am I Stressing It So Much?
If your passion priority is aggressive and clear, you can still articulate and create the "New need" as a problem statement like Steve Jobs did. Yes, there was no burning need to have a delicate touch mobile phone since people don't know what they want. He showed his passion statement to simplify people's lives. So, he has created a "New need" and created a new market. This became a burning need out of his "passion priority". So, your "strong passion" or "strong why" can lead to inventing new things and create strong need.

Alright, How Can You Make Sure that You Have Made a Fair Decision from Multiple Interests?

No confusion if you have one passion. However, if you, like me, have multiple passions, confusion is inevitable. It's natural, you're not alone. Not to worry…

> **"Our evolution stems from confronting doubts and moving through life's uncertainties from childhood,"**

Let me guide you in understanding about fairness of your decision. Think of a scene, eyes closed, where you enjoyed exceptional coffee or tea. Alright, now let's close this book and describe how amazing the coffee experience was.

Did you smell the aroma? Great, how was it? Was it tasty, rich, smooth, and strong?
This is the common perception of a good cup of coffee/tea. Are you genuinely interested in understanding the other effects of this very tasty coffee or tea?

> "The very first **Sip** of **the great coffee** will make you **forget anything** and **everything** at present **and reminisce** about something from **the past** or **future** memory to mind, leaving an **everlasting impression** in **your heart along with the aroma and taste!**"

A great coffee or tea equals a great experience! After the first sip, you are not with the coffee, it will take you into your dream world.

Similarly, once you have identified the right topic and start acting, you will find yourself in a similar state of mind. A topic that is near to your heart will do the following magic:

- It helps effortlessly shift focus away from other less interesting topics.
- It helps to surrender to the topic. You will find yourself immersed and filled with joy as you carry out the task.
- You will become so engrossed in it that time will fly by unnoticed.
- You will be as excited as a child during execution.
- Upon waking, feel excited as you ask yourself, "What action can I take today to progress on this topic?" So, your creative engine will be already in full gear.

If you observe these behavioral changes in yourself, it means you have already made the right choice! So, let's experience these existing moments.

What Is the Source of Motivation For a Few Well-known Personalities?

"The purpose of life is not to be happy. It is to be useful, honorable, compassionate, and have it make some difference that you have lived"

~Ralf Waldo Emerson

Following iconic people has a big passion as their goal. If you look at each of these passionate targets, **they're attached to a noble cause**. This helps to identify their "strong why". With a strong "why", nothing can hinder your pursuit of what you want.

Steve Jobs had an internal burning passion for creating innovative products that could change how people live and work.

A deep sense of service, a passion for education, and a commitment to scientific innovation motivated Dr. A.P.J. Abdul Kalam, the renowned scientist and former president of India.

One of the highly respected entrepreneurs, Mr. Ratan Tata, is motivated by a commitment to ethical leadership. He has emphasized the importance of conducting business with integrity, transparency, and fairness, setting high ethical standards for the Tata Group and the industry.

Robert Bosch, in doing business, was his persistent commitment to engineering excellence. A passion for innovation and technology deeply motivated Bosch. His dedication to producing high-quality, reliable products to improve lives is a central driving force in his business philosophy.

As founder of the Ford Motor Company, Henry Ford is credited as a pioneer in making "automobiles affordable for middle-class Americans.". The famous Model T [2] car was produced for 19 years, from 1908 to 1927, and almost 15 million units were made.

It put America on wheels and so changed the way Americans worked, lived, and played! Just look at the enormous indirect benefit of economic growth when there is an affordable transport mechanism available. Shopping malls, motels, planned suburbs with affordable housing, well-paid manufacturing jobs, and an emerging middle class eager to enjoy the perks of prosperity — this was modern, 20th-century America, and the Model T helped create it all.

If you examine great leaders, you'll find that they have clear and compelling reasons for improving people's lives as their core vision. At the heart of their mission is a noble cause, with personal gain taking a secondary role. It's a win-win situation—seeing others succeed is their true aspiration, and this journey brings them fulfillment. As mentioned before, profits, recognition, and accolades are simply side effects of this greater purpose.

> ***"Anything is possible under the roof of the sky, if you clearly understand your strong why with a serving mindset"***

Let's assume you aspire to become a CTO or CEO. The right mission includes growing the organization, creating numerous job opportunities through your hard work, increasing profitability, and contributing to the country's growth under your leadership—a clear win-win. In the same way, start working on your own targeted aspirations with similar goals to create a win-win scenario. This approach will naturally guide you to focus on building the functional, technical, and leadership skills needed to turn your dream into reality. These principles are the foundation of your success. With strong principles, you become unstoppable!

If you excel in electronics, why not begin anew, and gain the skills to create something beneficial for society? Why not start fresh and learn the skills needed to develop a drone with AI capability for multiple applications? Alternatively, you could explore a more innovative endeavor by teaching this skill to others.

If you find joy and inspiration in diving into the imaginative worlds of fiction novels, why not embark on the journey of creating one yourself? Your passion for storytelling could lead to the creation of captivating narratives that not only fulfill your own creative aspirations but also resonate with readers around the world.

If you are in the teaching field, why not make animation stories using AI tools and educate through creative ways of teaching complex topics online?

If you are a leader, why not share secrets of your success and tricks or coach or mentor those struggling in their career? As a leader, you possess a wealth of knowledge and experience gained through your journey to success. Why not take it forward by sharing your valuable insights, strategies, and mentorship with those who are navigating their career challenges? Your guidance and support could be the catalyst for their growth and success, fostering a culture of learning and development within your organization.

Happiness comes from achieving personal success, but fulfillment comes from bringing joy to others. Design your life in two stages: first, achieve happiness for yourself. Then, create a ripple effect to find true fulfillment. Remember, there is no such thing called failure—only lessons. Use those lessons to guide others, helping them avoid the same pitfalls and achieve outstanding success. This is the greatest fulfilling achievement for you!

"Ability does not matter here; it matters only a willingness to be kind enough and permitting oneself to share the knowledge or success with compassion that impact at scale."

My dream is to see a hunger-free world! I wish not to see a single beggar on the street. It is a shame for humanity to see a co-life begging for food. We witnessed a world desperate for knowledge and content. Now, it is freely available everywhere. Similarly, we should wipe off hunger from this world. Until then, I considered that our education system forgets to teach what genuine success is and will never meet its purpose! Let's strive together to change this situation.

I humbly request that you do not simply work for promotion or run a business just for profit. One fine day, this will make you stand empty. Attach your compassionate mindset to serve the misfortune of others as your acute vision.

Please do not misunderstand that the primary focus is not to become popular. If you become popular, it is just a side effect. The primary goal is to draw a sensational passion and live with inner peace and joy.

Determine to become an influencing leader or businessperson, "to speak for voiceless" and there you will move with new mindset, strategies and feel the sense of attainment of your purpose and joyfulness like all other influential leaders!

A Research Study Outcome

Our knowledge about the factors that contribute to an individual's fulfillment and success from a psychological perspective is currently insufficient. Researchers on this topic conducted multiple research projects. One of the famous research projects conducted by L. Nash H. Stevenson [9] on 1 Feb 2004 with hundreds of professionals to study the assumptions behind the idea of it.

Pursuing success can feel like shooting in a landscape of moving targets: Every time you hit one, five more pop up from another direction. **We are under constant pressure to do, get, and be more**. Is that truly the essence of success?

They created a practical framework for redefining success, leading to personal and professional fulfillment, not anxiety or stress.

The authors' research uncovered four unavoidable components of fulfillment:

- **Happiness** (feelings of pleasure or contentment about your life)

- **Achievement** (accomplishments that compare favorably against similar goals others have strived for);

- **Significance** (the sense that you've made a positive impact on people you care about)

- **Legacy** (a way to establish your values or accomplishments to help others find future success).

Unless you are consistently hitting on all four categories, it is impossible to be satisfied with any win.

People who achieve lasting success tend to rely on a kaleidoscope strategy to structure their aspirations and activities. This article explains how to build your kaleidoscope framework. The process can help you determine which tasks you should undertake to fulfill the different components of success and uncover areas where there are holes.

It can also help you make better choices about what you spend your time on and the energy level you put into each activity. According to Nash and Stevenson, successful people who experience absolute satisfaction achieve it by deliberately imposing limits. Cultivating your sense of "just enough" can help you set reachable goals, tally up more true wins, and enjoy lasting success.

Many people will generally reach the first two elements, "happiness" and "Achievement". However, this gives temporary excitement because of much applause from the external world. It fades in a matter of days, weeks, or months, leaving emptiness until the next win.

Yes, you will return to square one until try another success story since now you need the same excitement repeatedly. This is an addiction until you realize it.

If you look at some people's money-earning mentality, they travel through various stages. Initially, they feel I have no money, then they move to I have less money, then I have not enough money, then again, I have no colossal money. This journey of self-trap and worry never ends for no reason! People do not even know why they earn so much; it becomes an addiction, and they are very busy in getting more money than living this moment.

You can be very aggressive and ambitious until you reach your success and happiness. There is no shortcut. If you require this ambitious achievement and happiness to remain for your entire life, move your character to be more polite, kind in parallel while you are moving for the next win. What systematic actions can you take to cultivate politeness and kindness?

- Make sure all your achievements made a big impact. Inspired to change many lives.

- Focus on helping people to find their future from your experience through mentoring.

So, achievement will bring hype for you. It'll fade from memory. The key to launching into a fulfilling life lies in building trust through delivering value and consistently uplifting others. Your account will be flooded with hearts!

The Transformation from Consumer to Creator Mindset

We use a lot of products in our daily life. Every day, every minute, we use many products from the Internet, social media, mobile phones, cars, bikes, flights, and more and more. Every product made out here was from someone else big dream. Whether it is small or big, it changed our life the way we live today. So, we consume more than we create.

Steve Jobs conveys this message in his famous Stanford University speech: "Your regular job or business is filling up most of your day. Fulfillment requires executing with elegance. It is only possible when done with heartfulness. Until you get this type of work, don't stop searching..."

Why does Steve Jobs push to search for work or business until you execute with elegance? You run the task elegantly since it comes from the heart and is part of your intrinsic motivation. Creativity and innovation are sisters and brothers when inherent motivation exists in your activities. They come along naturally. You will start applying new ideas, new ways of executing and designing, using contemporary techniques, and entirely fresh surprises as outcomes.

If you look around, exceptionally few lucky people will identify their passionate topic early in their age. Is it true? No, their supporting environment helped them to get this clarity in an early stage, not based on luck. This is the right reason. The majority are not born with luck or super brains. (there could be a few rare exceptions)

Let's look at a funny example. Let's assume you were born in the Stone Age. What would be your dress? You would likely create your dress from materials such as animal hides, furs, or woven plant fibers. What would be your daily job? Learning all tricks to hunt and hunt animals. Is that all you've learned in your entire life?

Imagine being a person from the stone age suddenly waking up in a modern apartment. Tell me now, what would be your state of mind? How do you feel? You look at everything around as awkward,right?

This is exactly what happens to you! If someone is intelligent and makes wonderful decisions, they would have lived in a knowledgeable environment and have granted easy access to learn from there. When you compare their growth might be much farther from your growth. You are not the cause and do not blame your ability and knowledge. Your initial environment design, which was not in your control, made you stay away from such knowledge!

It is not your mistake to be born into an environment that has not provided enough knowledge, and there is absolutely NO SHAME in it. But IF YOU CONTINUE TO BE THERE, IT IS YOUR REAL PROBLEM!

Taking small steps to change your surroundings can provide you with the clarity needed to determine the best approach for achieving your goals. Surrounding yourself with intelligent and successful people. They will inspire you to make intelligent life plans. Shift your perspective from being a "consumer" to becoming a "creator" by changing your environment. Finding the right environment depends on the topic you choose and how passionate you are about it.

Branding the Authenticity [Identity Creation]

For any product you buy from the market, you always pay higher if it is a well-known brand. The brand is a trust. Branding comes with some key differentiators and uniqueness.

A car company produces many models without naming each model uniquely, and one particular model delivered this year is exemplary. How will the positive word of mouth communicate to others, which will help to increase the sales drastically, if no unique model name is available?

So, brand draws authenticity. This also applies to people. Otherwise, every hard work goes unnoticed if not gathered under one brand.

This is quite clear in business. How do I create my brand if I am working for a company? OK, let me tell you about my small experience. After finishing a detailed training on a technical topic, I was supporting a project to solve technical issues when raised from large customers base. I consistently offered support, but my work went unnoticed because I delivered nothing independently. If there is an escalation, people will look for my help. So, I am known for negative reasons. This means I am appreciated only when I solve any serious escalation.

So, it has become like a doctor's job. If no one gets a disease, doctors will go bankrupt. Thinking everyone should get a disease is a bad idea. Similarly, waiting for escalation is unappreciated. It started bothering me and creates a negative mindset.

Solution? Just try to escape from this role and switch to a different topic where people acknowledge and appreciate your contribution for any product development. Unfortunately, I must leave this valuable knowledge behind for selfish reasons.

But I spent some time contemplating my decision before making it. For every problem, there must exist more than one solution with a win-win option. But it requires two elements to find the new alternative, they are, a **positive mindset** and **proactive thinking**.

How do you apply these two elements in this context? In the medical field, you can develop a preventive mechanism to defend against diseases and guide people on effectively preventing them, minimizing the risk to life and promoting quick patient recovery.

Using the same two elements, I have decided to develop a product idea (Framework) that addresses every issue from our collective experience. With this idea, our team pitched funding requests, and it was seen as something that will prevent issues, save effort, be state-of-the-art, and help position the team well with quality goals. Due to its merit, the pitch got approved.

My team started developing it and promoting the use of this product instead of solving their nail-biting issues directly. We named and designed logs, created punch words, and marketed it. So, this product became my brand. So, whatever topic you work on, look at the big picture, consolidate, create (it could even be a document solution), and call it "Your name's- Magic theory or solution" It will gain traction! After gaining authenticity, branding is so important that people will remember you. This should create a positive vibe.

So, check your current scenario, if these two elements can be applied in your area (in your business or profession) and just try it out to proactively provide a solution to your customers and at the same time establish your identity. Win-win is a continues practice.

How does Identity Create a Brand and Boost Self-Confidence?

Asking about someone's identity might cause a puzzling expression. It's an odd question because we rarely think. When we try to explain, we struggle for an answer. Nevertheless, we all have an identity.

What identify can do for an individual? This identity significantly shapes our actions and, ultimately, our life outcomes. People go to great lengths to match their actions with their sense of self.

Mr. Darren Gold, a Former Forbes Council member, explained [5] his coaching experience with senior leaders. He has been fixated on understanding what sets average performance apart from exceptional performance. It turns out that identity plays a crucial role. Take the top performers in sports and the arts. Nearly everyone saw themselves as extraordinary even before having proof. They firmly believed in their greatness, which was ingrained in their identity.

Additionally, he provides a real-life iconic example of Muhammad Ali's life. He didn't just see himself as a great boxer; he proclaimed himself the "king of the world." He didn't hide his confidence and was not shy about sharing this identity. Consequently, his actions and results naturally reflected this identity, leaving a profound impact far beyond the boxing ring and influencing global culture.

He asked a critical question that makes us think so deeply, "***So if everyone has an identity, and if that identity is a crucial driver of human behavior, wouldn't it make sense to choose an identity that is most likely to get the results you want in life?*** "

This book is all about discovering your next version by identity from your chosen topic suited and decided by you!

o------o

Chapter 4: Clarity-How to Choose a Topic: Key Takeaways

Losing focus on a selected topic is common diseases. Not only interest but valuable time fall into the trap of distraction due to other attractions. We select another topic and this cycle repeats. It is important to understand the reason before it is too late. Most of the time, we choose any topics based on the influence of the trend or hype in the external environmental attraction. Alternatively, if the topic chosen is based on intrinsic motivation, then it is your real passion. Once done, real life starts, and it enables us to stay focused despite distractions.

Here, there were ten different techniques explained to identify your passion. So, before starting exercise, settle into a peaceful environment and your high productive time, to maximize focus. With a clear mind, recall moments of profound satisfaction or happiness, jotting them down under the column titled "My Passion." Next, delve into childhood memories, unearthing aspirations and inspirations that may have faded over time. Just capture it as well.

As you continue, reflect on unforeseen challenges you've confronted and how you navigated through them. Consider the lessons learned and the potential to share these insights with others through structured programs or online coaching. Tap into your areas of expertise, whether technical skills or leadership abilities, to develop impactful solutions or training programs.

Finally, revisit a long list of aspirations or life goals that may have been sidelined by circumstance, brainstorming small actionable steps to reignite their pursuit. Through this process of reflection, ideation and choosing the right topic to start with priority, you'll unearth a wealth of potential avenues to explore in pursuit of your life dream project.

Passionate leaders like Steve Jobs, Dr. A.P.J. Abdul Kalam, Ratan Tata, Robert Bosch, and Henry Ford are driven by noble causes, reflecting a deep commitment to improving lives. They exemplify the importance of a strong "why" behind their endeavors, with service and innovation as core motivations. Their pursuit of noble causes brings them fulfillment and joy, with profit and recognition being mere side effects of their impactful work. Determine to become an influencing leader or businessperson, "to speak for voiceless" and there you will unlock your New You!

The research study conducted by Nash and Stevenson highlights the insufficiency of our understanding of fulfillment and success from a psychological perspective. They propose a framework comprising happiness, achievement, significance, and legacy as essential components of fulfillment, emphasizing the importance of hitting on all four categories for lasting satisfaction. Ultimately, the key lies in delivering value, uplifting others, and making a positive impact on people's lives.

Establishing authenticity through branding is crucial, be it for products or individuals. Without a unique brand, hard work might go unnoticed, as seen in my personal experiences.

Identity forms the core of personal branding, shaping actions and outcomes. Darren Gold [5] highlights how identity distinguishes average from exceptional performance, citing Muhammad Ali's bold self-proclamation as "king of the world." Embracing a chosen identity aligned with desired outcomes is emphasized for personal growth and success.

Chapter 5: Setting up Internal Infrastructure

****

"If I believe I can do it, I shall surely acquire the capacity to do it even if I may not have it at the beginning."

~Mahatma Gandhi

You've got your passion statement locked in. Now, get ready for execution with what value you will deliver and how it would impact at scale. Alright, before directly jumping into action, just pause for a moment and learn all the following listed techniques to prepare your mindset required during execution.

The Brain Exercises to Break the Pattern and Create New Neural Pathways

Creativity is more important when you execute tasks aligned with your goals. Every innovation and creativity come out of a different thinking pattern. Can this be learned? Yes, of course, by training the brain.

Let's start with a simple exercise to break the pattern of a daily routine. You drive to your office location by following a regular route daily. Begin a bit earlier and attempt to discover different paths to the same destination using a map, without relying on a navigation system. Attempt to notice any new things that are available along your newly identified travel route (ex: new shops, showrooms) and try to memorize what you have seen, which might be interesting to you.

If you observe, you might be curious, surprised, and a little annoyed, and overall, it will give you a pleasant experience if you successfully find an alternative route! It instantly creates a happy mind. Happiness will extend to other activities without your notice in your day. Even if you do not succeed, it creates a satisfaction for the experiment followed by curiosity to find another route the next day.

Conversely, what is occurring within our brain system? By experimenting with small additional activities and cultivating new behaviors, a fresh neural pathway is formed. It is important to repeat and practice the new activities to help the pathway strengthen with the number of times the brain cells "fire" to conduct the new activity.

It refers to your brain's ability to restructure or rewire itself when recognizing the need for adaptation. In other words, it can continue to develop and change throughout life. Small adventures refresh the mind and enhance memory.

Similarly, starting cycling, exercising, hearing new music, learning a new language are a few more examples of developing brain muscles.

These small brain exercises are just the beginning. This will slowly boost up your confident level higher and you need to raise the bar in taking bigger exercise like betting for high ticket closing in business scenario, if you are a business person or trying to take up a high-risk roles if you are an employee in an organization, etc., I assure, you will experience a lot of surprises on your high ability once you face the situation.

Pause to Generate New Energy and Remove Brain Toxic Technique

First, pause the current routine, find your peace, take a break, and go to an idle state. Every innovation or new idea originates from an idle situation. We have seen this proven multiple times. Einstein had just noticed the apple dropping from the tree and discovered gravity when he was sitting idle.

Idle means giving a break to your brain from other worries and tasks. During this time, the brain moves to default function mode and tries to make a new neurons connection. This happens only during idle mode. We hardly have a chance to experience from our daily routine.

Find your calm place, preferably early morning, and give your mind space to enjoy stillness for 10 to 15 minutes daily. Live with yourself, free from thoughts. It's tough to stay like this, isn't it? The moment you sit down, all wanted and unwanted things will flow into the mind. Escape from these thoughts by following simple tricks.

- Have a clean floor mat and sit down on the floor in a calm place where you get fresh air. Close your eyes and focus to watch the sound of your breath (deep inhale) and feel the refreshing oxygen go into your body and spread from lungs to each organ of your body. Let's feel every molecule of pure oxygen flow into your body to give great energy. Just feel and enjoy it repeatedly.

Try practicing it, starting with only for 3 minutes on the first day and increase up to 10 or 15 minutes every day. This will keep you more active for the entire day. After a few days, as soon as you sit down and close your eyes, the brain effortlessly switches into autopilot mode to do this activity. Once you reach this state, you will be in idle mode. You will not realize it, but you will be!

When you're overwhelmed by worries, fear, or negative thoughts, try following simple trick for instant relief. If you're seeking immediate relief from feeling weighed down, this method is perfect for you:

- If negative thoughts emerge, find a comfortable place to sit, close your eyes, and imagine a glowing candle right in front of you. Feel the radiance emitted by the candle. Catch each of your evil thoughts (anger, cheating, unfair act by someone, some pain created because of situation, failures, wrong decisions, frustration) and drop into the candle flame.

Just see it has burnt and a little smoke exhale. So, the first pain is gone away from you. Try to continue until you put all your bad emotional thoughts into this candle flame and just burn it to smoke. After this exercise, you will feel so much freedom from these evil thoughts. If you sense a heaviness in your heart, make sure to remind yourself to repeat this exercise.

Sleep to Repair Technique

Why do we need to sleep? People often think that sleep is just "down time," when a tired brain gets to rest, said Dr. Maiken Nedergaard, who studies sleep at the University of Rochester.

"But that's wrong," she said. While you sleep, your brain is working. For example, sleep helps prepare your brain to learn, remember, and create.

Nedergaard and her colleagues discovered that the brain has a drainage system that removes toxins during sleep.

"When we sleep, the brain totally changes function," she explained. "It becomes almost like a kidney, removing waste from the system."

Her team found in mice that the drainage system removes some proteins linked with Alzheimer's disease. The drainage system removed these toxins twice as fast from the brain during sleep.

Everything from blood vessels to the immune system uses sleep as a time for repair, says [3] Dr. Kenneth Wright, Jr., a sleep researcher at the University of Colorado.

"There are certain repair processes that occur in the body mostly, or most effectively, during sleep," he explained. "If you don't get enough sleep, those processes are going to be disturbed."

Understand that transitioning to the next version can be initially stressful. Yes, it will be. But it is an investment. If things shift the way you want after your consistent effort, will it turn out to be pleasant? Each day, hour, and minute will be unforgettable and enjoyable. Your productivity will bring happiness. Your loved ones foster a positive mindset from your nice behaviors. So, it is an investment to identify your pleasantness.

14 Secrets to Prepare Winning Mindset

"You will find it easier to be successful if you first know what you are. Next, you must plan to take action to get started. You will not likely know all the answers when you start, but you must not let that prevent you from beginning your success journey."

~Don M. Green, Executive Director
Napoleon Hill Foundation

1. Most people will fail after some progress since they do not initially set up their basic internal infrastructure. Building basic infrastructure means preparing your mind, like getting prepared for the war zone. Before getting into a war zone, a lot of preparations are required addressing from safety to survival aspects. Preparation of your mindset requires a similar thought process. Please understand this approach deeply. Jumping into the field with just your passion alone, without proper preparation, will likely send you right back to square one.

    Start with your strategies. Think about the key approaches needed to achieve your goals. For example, if you want to become a singer, break down the journey into stages—basic, intermediate, and advanced singing abilities. For each level, define the specific actions required, from learning the fundamentals to building your personal brand. This structured approach will guide you step-by-step towards your desired results.

2. Our brains are always busy with thoughts and information. It needs a break too. Taking breaks improves attention, motivation, productivity, creativity, and memory. Giving your brain a break doesn't mean it stops working completely, give a time removes its toxic chemicals.

Dr Kunal Bahrani, director of neurology at Fortis Escorts Hospital Faridabad, explains, a well-rested brain feels refreshed and focused. It helps you make better decisions, stay calm in challenges, and stabilize your emotions. So, taking breaks is not just good for your brain, but it is crucial for feeling better and thinking clearly.

Different format of breaks: A good night's deep sleep, a minimum of 1/2 hour of physical exercise (at least a brisk walk), eating when you feel hunger, mindful minor breaks, digital detox, social interaction, a wonderful vacation.

Here, a digital detox is something important that, as explained in the earlier chapter, requires a reduction of screen time and conscious monitoring daily. Try to switch off all app notifications. This is difficult; try it out; it gives great relief and gives you more time. Schedule a constant duration for screen time and adhere to your own rules.

3. A systematic approach and discipline yield better results than unstructured execution. To achieve success, follow a systematic approach that outlines goals, training, resources, and time commitments, including your breaks.

   Learning this importance in a systematic approach is a well-proven method. As you notice, right from the school teaching system to achieving big organizational goals, everything works under a well-defined system. Make your personalized daily, weekly, and monthly schedule and targets and stick to it.

4. If you planned to take part in a soccer match tomorrow morning, you should have taken all your sports belongings ready the previous night, prepared for sound sleep, going to bed thinking of various scenarios such as what kind of situation will arise during the match and how to toggle it, etc. Mentally, you have fully prepared yourself with eagerness, energy, and confidence. A similar approach needs to be applied while executing your chosen topic. Start like every day is like your first day of execution in your mission.

5. Before you go to bed, take a moment to visualize your target in as much detail as possible—imagine

how it will feel and look once you've achieved it. This vivid mental image is like uploading an assignment into your brain. By doing this, you unlock the incredible power of your subconscious mind. The next morning, your brain will start offering new ideas and solutions related to this goal. The deeper you immerse yourself in this visualization, the more powerful, the results will be. I've personally experienced many times.

6. Write down your first target for becoming your next version, like a vision statement, in a handy notebook, follow the format provided below. The purpose of this vision statement is to read it daily. Now, let's try writing your own personalized version. Customize and replace the underlined sections in the following paragraph with your own unique vision:

I commit to becoming the next version of "*Your New Target Version*" by following these "*Learning Methods*" and dedicating "*n Hours*" each day, along with "*n Hours*" on weekends. I will immediately apply all my learnings through "*These Actions*" to achieve my "*Dream Target*" by "*This Date.*"

Now, you know how many days you have left from today to achieve your dream of a new version. Divide your total available days into small milestones for minor achievements.

For example, plan a few milestones like 1. Learning, 2. hands-on tryout, 3. solving first level problem, 4. showcasing intermediate solution, 5. writing an article and posting a blog, 6. preparing for test run and mocks and 7. Deliver final product/service. So, plan your milestones according to your action item with a definite target date.

This applies to anything and everything, whether you want to deliver a product or become CEO or CTO. So, the action item might vary depending on your choice of target but break it into small milestones and execute with a clear target and celebrate every small milestone on successful completion!

Here, declaring the final date is mandatory; otherwise, the entire show won't work out. The importance of setting a target date is that if you cannot meet a smaller goal along the way, feel a sense of urgency and make up for it before the next milestone, making no compromises.

7. Now, build your own rules. For example, if you miss out on a daily commitment, it should accumulate over the weekend. Now, I do not miss out on daily obligations. OK, I missed one day during the week, so you must declare and compromise on Sunday.

So, create your own rules and ensure that you cannot escape from progressing every week strongly. You are the best person who can close all these loopholes with your own rules! This will create your discipline, which I call here a system to achieve your destiny. Following all the tips will help shape your discipline.

8. Once you decide on a goal to achieve, focus anything and everything towards achieving this goal with no second thought and do not allow any other inspiration to move you away. Just focus on this **One thing**, as Bruce Lee said,

"I fear not the man who has practiced 10,000 kicks once, but I fear the man who has practiced one kick 10,000 times."
— Bruce Lee

9. Any significant achievements will start from the first baby step. So, consistency and practice are the key. So, prepare your mindset that you will not go to bed without small action taken towards target.

"Everyone wants to learn how to win, but no one wants to *learn*." If you're addicted to social media, that's okay—just make it work for you. Follow and subscribe to content that aligns with your passion but focus solely on the *one* chosen topic you're committed to mastering. Be addict to what you really want. Use it as a tool to learn more and take action.

This is equal to turning your FM radio into the right station where "you hear only what you want to hear." Another critical step that I have learned is that too much information will float, but carefully take notes into a small physical pocket notebook (I mean it) where you will consciously revisit at the start of the next day to apply this learning.

10. It is very normal to feel frustrated, bored, or demotivated, etc. when you execute your dream project. It even applies to famous scientists. But how do you get motivation? It is a very simple trick. Just get into the task for that day, irrespective of your mood. If you begin to execute, automatic motivation comes along. It seems to be a very crazy hint, but this will work exceptionally well.

Stephen King, a famous author who sold 30 million copies of his books, was asked in one the interview, "How did you get motivated and flow to write these many books?" He said, "Just start writing, you will get motivation."

There is no need for any external motivation; the mind works amazingly; if you simply start involving your activity for the day, and you tend to forget your current mood after a few minutes. You will be in your own world. You never even noticed that you have already got the motivation. You will be busy with it.

11. If you start anything new, initially, it appears like a mountain in front of you. It appears like many achievers could finish it with ease of time. Do they have a time machine? It is a widespread feeling during execution, especially when mastering a new topic. Be patient but progress without leaving hope.

    Successful individuals dedicate years to hard work and practice for their dreams. We see only the tip of the iceberg - their results, not the effort. If you want to energize self or move away from a down mood, try to visualize the result you want to achieve and you will immediately get excited to work on your topic.

    How does doing it minimally each day significantly impact my life? A plane changing one-degree slight right turn in the sky seems to have no significant effect; if this one degree is consistently maintained, based on the speed, the plane will reach a few miles away from its original path after one hour! After 10 hours, it will reach a different place than the target destination. A consistent habit of acting can transform you into an expert within a year on any subject.

12. Motivation. The passionate target is chosen by you based on internal calling and not by an external

force. It is fueled by intrinsic motivation and does not depend on external factors. Watching a variety of motivational videos regularly is like continuously using different drugs to keep you high. This drug will not allow you to focus on your ONE topic. You can watch it if you feel low to get some energy and be aware of your limit.

The world is moving towards becoming more competitive. The formula inspired by others is no longer effective. Let's try not to live someone else's life. In the long run, it won't sustain; hence, listen to inner calling. This will turn you amazingly to take consistent action with a "no matter what" mindset. Your enthusiasm for the outcome makes every execution step alluring, devoid of external motivation.

13. Partially declare (without giving complete information) to a few well-wishers that you will do something with some target date. For example, if you decided to direct a movie, just declare it, "I am directing a documentary movie that is expected to be released in 3 months." Keep the rest of all secret remain with you and surprise everyone with a big bang when you release it.

Here's the trick: when you hint about your project, you raise expectations and others will keep tabs on you. So, you are creating an artificial push to yourself by others. When meeting the same person, they will eagerly ask about your release plans, igniting your passion and sense of responsibility. You will focus more and avoid any deviation from the commitment.

This is the exact trick film producers will do. They create big publicity and hype to the public with trailer with release date. The director will automatically feel the enormous responsibility lying in front of him and push him to meet commitment.

Give it a shot with your own creation. This creates little artificial pressure, but it is positive pressure for your growth.

14. How do you keep yourself energized? Keep your energy level up by celebrating every milestone with a small gathering and sharing the joy with family and friends. Just repeat each small milestone as a habit to motivate you! Find a self-gifting mechanism. Just take an internal pledge that after finishing 50% of my work, let me self-gift a good momentum. This mechanism is a great energy drink for you and has a dual benefit. You're on the target and you get your self-gift.

Chapter 5: Setting up Internal Infrastructure: Key Takeaways

In order to play soccer match, a good stadium is needed. Similarly, it is imperative to construct a solid mental infrastructure before diving into the game of life. Here is the step-by-step process to prepare your mindset involves recognizing the importance of mental preparation, breaking pattern for more creativity, taking breaks for better brain function, incorporating healthy habits like sleep and exercise, practicing digital detox, and creating a systematic approach to goal achievement.

To foster creativity and improve risk taking ability, break few routine patterns. Engage the brain with simple training that form **new neural pathways**. Start by exploring alternative routes to familiar destinations, memorizing new sights along the way.

Try to notice the curiosity and satisfaction that comes with discovering new paths, which will strengthen the brain's ability to adapt and change.

Additionally, often try out with any small new activity introduced consistently activities like changing to new paste, learning to brush with left hand, start cycling, new exercise, learning a new language etc., These small steps will further develop cognitive abilities and boost confidence in all activities.

Pause to create idle moments for the brain. This Idle mode is called Brain's default function mode. During this time, **it tries to make new neurons connection**.

It is a wonderful exercise to get out of box ideas. Find a peaceful space, preferably in the morning, to sit, focus on breath sound and feel fresh oxygen energies each part of your body. Gradually increase the duration up to 10 or 15 minutes. This gives great energy and new thoughts.

To get an instant relief from evil thoughts, follow this exercise: Visualize a glowing candle and release negative emotions into its flame. Each emotional burden will disappear like smoke from a flame, leaving you with a sense of relief. Regularly practice these techniques to maintain mental freedom and emotional well-being.

14 approaches to prepare your mindset to achieve success are explained here. Preparing your mindset is more important than executing to stay consistent, it's crucial to understand your goals and devise actionable plans to achieve them.

Taking regular breaks is essential for refreshing your brain and maintaining focus. Adopting a systematic approach with discipline ensures better results, similar to preparing for a sports match.

Breaking down your goals into achievable milestones and adhering to your own rules fosters consistency and progress. Focus solely on your chosen goal to avoid distractions and stay on track. Starting with small steps and maintaining consistency is key, even when feeling demotivated.

Visualizing success and finding intrinsic motivation are vital for staying motivated in the long run. Additionally, sharing goals partially can create positive pressure and accountability, while celebrating milestones and self-rewarding helps to maintain energy and motivation throughout the journey.

Conclusion

"Every sunset is an opportunity to reset. Every sunrise begins with new eyes."

-RICHIE NORTEN

And this brings us to the end of this book.

Now that you understand the fundamental difference between your current mindset and fully prepared to develop your ultimate new mindset with a deep understanding of yourself.

After trying out certain practical exercises with a different mindset, you will be surprised and proud to see yourself. Since you are well aware of many techniques that can support you in **designing your own strategies**, and easily handle challenges in different areas of your life.

I wrote this book with the intention that you could seamlessly apply its techniques as you read through. **I trust you've made time to engage with the exercises**, and if so, I believe you've already felt a surge in confidence, guiding you toward recognizing "**Your Deeper Inside**" as first winning and a foundation for external success.

Believe me, once you have identified your inner calling (genuine passion), you cannot measure your excitement. This is only the beginning. If you start to be preparing your mind based on these deep understanding, automatically you will get a fair idea on where to begin to write your success story. If yes, you will be one of happiest and satisfied human in the earth.

Some people prefer grasping the full concept before diving into practise. If that's you, no sweat! Now that you've read through, it's time to circle back to the exercises and witness the changes for yourself.

To give you a swift rundown, I've summarized all the main ideas from each chapter into summaries at the end of each one. This way, you can easily grasp the essence of the content at a glance, getting a bird's-eye view of the material.

As you apply these techniques in your life, remember to share some of your minor success or technique with nears and dears. By helping others, you initiate a ripple effect, fostering a world where people support one another and thrive together. I am eagerly awaiting to read your success story.

I wish for you to uncover a magnificent NEW YOU, brimming with joy, abundance, satisfaction, and fulfilment. May your life attract boundless success, drawn by the gravity of your extraordinary journey!

Cheers

May I ask you for a small favor?

One last time! **I'd love if you could leave a review about the book**. Reviews may not matter to big-name authors; but they're a tremendous help for authors like me, who don't have much following, and this is my first book.

They help me to grow my readership by encouraging folks to take a chance on my books. To put it straight–reviews are the life blood for any author. **It is the sole means of connecting you and me**. Please leave your review by clicking the link below, it will directly lead you to the book review page.

PLEASE VISIT DIRECT CUSTOMER REVIEW LINK OF "*WIN INSIDE TO WIN OUTSIDE*"

It will just take less than a minute of yours but will tremendously help me to reach out to more people, so please leave your review. Thank you for supporting my work and I'd love to see your review of the book.

Full Book Summary

Chapter 1-Introduction: Key Takeaways

Winning: It brings excitement, confidence, and success, but it also introduces the fear of maintaining that success. People are captivated by success stories because they associate winning with self-esteem, happiness, and security. However, winning is not a permanent state; it is a journey that requires preparation and mental conditioning. Like navigating a new city, success becomes easier with practice and familiarity, but it starts with building the right mindset.

The foundation of consistent winning: It lies in a strong, adaptable mindset. Each challenge should be approached with the intensity of a first timer, always prepared and innovating. Success is not solely about skill but consistency and breaking through mental barriers.

Understanding the purpose behind your drive to win is essential. This book will guide you on how to develop practical strategies, manage expectations, and cultivate a winning mindset to achieve lasting success in life and beyond.

Break old belief to crack your new version: A man passing an elephant camp saw adult elephants tied to small trees with thin ropes. Wondering why they didn't break free, he asked the trainer, who explained that young elephants are tied with these ropes and conditioned to believe they can't break them as they grow.

This story teaches us about the power of the mind; if we believe we're limited, we won't attempt to break free, even when we have the strength to do so.

You have full power to take a decision now: Your current state reflects the choices that brought you here, where many settle into a monotonous routine, unaware of the trap. Fortunately, you've made a wake-up call, seizing the chance to find purpose and fulfillment.

Let's explore the vibrant spectrum of life together, filled with growth, excitement, satisfaction, and success. Craft your own story, embracing joy and fulfillment to live an extraordinary life beyond boundaries.

Just pause from routine and reflect now: The daily grind encompasses a structured routine of responsibilities, leaving little room for introspection. Prioritizing the needs of others often takes precedence, leading to a cycle of monotony.

However, it's crucial to pause and reflect, asking probing questions to uncover deeper meaning and purpose. Embracing self-discovery and personal growth amidst the chaos can lead to a fulfilling and transformative journey toward fulfillment and financial independence.

Realize you live in emptiness: In the reality of life, small victories like promotions or business successes provide fleeting satisfaction, leading to a constant cycle of seeking temporary fulfillment. This pattern, known as the "emptiness cycle," leaves little room for sustained joy and satisfaction, with 80% to 90% of our time spent in this state.

Despite the rapid passage of time, few PAUSE to reflect or plan for lasting satisfaction, prioritizing external achievements over inner fulfillment. It's essential to ask listed deeper questions about our purpose and achievements, beyond material success, to find true happiness and satisfaction in life.

Preventing you from regrets: This book offers a comprehensive guide to personal growth and development, focusing on various aspects such as purpose identification, overcoming limiting beliefs, enhancing relationships, building self-esteem for a successful grand life with abundant of wealth.

Chapter 2- Right Questions and Basic Understanding: Key Takeaways

Ask a few mindful questions to understand self: This chapter encourages deep reflection on life's purpose and priorities, urging to consider aspirations and seize opportunities. Through the listed thought-provoking questions, it emphasizes the value of taking risks and pursuing dreams. Break free from routine and invest in personal growth and fulfilment, shaping a more meaningful future through introspection and action.

Discover your inner strength and overcome doubts: Two different situations are explained here. One involves running competitively for a big prize, while the other is about surviving a dangerous encounter in a forest. If anyone's effort is equal to the second situation, it is impossible to find any competitions around!

Learning from Jim Thorpe's story: It teaches us that challenges can't stop us if we tap into our full potential. By thinking like we're facing a life-or-death situation in everything we do, we can achieve incredible things. Practice this mindset daily to find deep satisfaction and success. Ask yourself key questions to unlock your full power and see amazing results in your life.

The brain does not allow us to take any risks and tricks to overcome: Based on the experience, the brain builds a belief system over the years. Whenever you try to break the belief system, that means taking some risk to gain some improvement.

Our brain finds it very uncomfortable since survival is the topmost priority for the brain system. So, it will constantly try to pull back to the safe zone. This is the core reason to continue the default life than moving to dream life. One should understand and need to break with very small risk-taking tasks consistently to **train the brain to build new mental muscles exactly like going to the gym** every day.

Imagine, you can: Our brains, like adaptable software, thrive on self-trust and dedication to learning. Gautama Buddha's wisdom underscores the transformative power of thought. Efficiently navigating today's information age is key amidst fear of change. Leveraging time and learning yields life's greatest wonders.

Excess and easy information is dangerous: When things become readily available, we often take them for granted, losing sight of their value. The overwhelming noise of information can cloud our judgment and distract us from our true selves. Consuming endless content without direction leaves us empty-handed, akin to listening to multiple songs at once. Our innocence and daily negligence can lead to significant long-term losses.

Effort required to build your next version: This is an ongoing journey towards purpose and fulfillment, not just a destination. Start with the 80/20 rule: allocate 80% to current responsibilities and invest 20% daily towards personal growth, gaining clarity as you progress.

Be proud of the gifts you already have: If I relate this here to this businessperson's story, we always think about what we don't have and feel low. I realize you have already given many gift cheques, such as "your body, your soul, your breath, your imagination, your freedom, learning ability, your health, your parents, your friends and so on and on." Realize priceless gifts already given for you to move forward with confidence to find your next version.

Chapter 3: Barrier Stones to Self-Discovery- Unlocking the New You: Key Takeaways

Limiting belief is like a mirage, deceiving and elusive. Chinese businessman seeking a successor to sell combs in a Buddhist monastery. Despite the initial skepticism, the third son proposes a creative idea— printing Buddha's teachings on combs. When people comb every time, they remember this teaching.

This innovative approach leads to significant sales. The key takeaways include breaking limiting beliefs, focusing on providing value to stakeholders, emphasizing compassion in mindset over mere sales, and emphasizing that where there is a will, there is a way. The story aims to challenge common limiting beliefs and self-doubts in individuals.

Here's a story from my own life. A while back, I shared a simple idea with a well-known a very small business owner that dramatically boosted his sales over a few years. He had been focused on increasing his customer base each month.

I suggested he pause and consider adding a new commodity by learning new knowledge about it to his portfolio, leveraging the trust he already had with existing customers. This approach allowed him to double his revenue without needing to find new customers.

So, this approach made him come out from a limiting belief of always running business in a traditional way. Since then, expanding his product line has become a key strategy in addition to adding additional customers for his business.

It is important to be brave enough to challenge your own deeply held beliefs. Let's take one sample question: What is preventing you from becoming a vice president of an organization? If you don't question yourself, your mind will be convinced it's not for you permanently.

It all starts with mindful questions. This book serves as a **life guide, empowering you to think, question, discover, transform, and, most importantly, create and share values** that **allow you to live the life you've always dreamed of.**

External forces influence our behavior and shape our identity, often unconsciously. Society's pressures to imitate or compete divert us from our authentic path, leading to temporary satisfaction but long-term disconnection from our true selves.

Emotions play a significant role in our reactions, often limiting our thinking and problem-solving abilities. However, by pausing, analyzing, and responding with maturity, we can transcend temporary fixes and address the root causes of our challenges.

Taking control of our responses empowers us to shape our own narrative, leaving behind past images and crafting a new, authentic version of ourselves.

Face the fear. A story about how a group of young lions devised a clever plan to catch gazelles by using the fear of older lions. It teaches to "run towards the roar," facing fears rather than avoiding them. Courage isn't the absence of fear but moving forward despite it. Being afraid of both failing and succeeding leads to a default life. Embracing challenges with courage defines true living.

How are you treating yourself every day? Imagine your younger self sitting opposite to you. It is unfair to tell him about his inability daily. If you **are not taking action to move forward, then understand that you are telling this to you every day** unconsciously. Instead, demonstrate your greatness by taking action towards success.

You're not meant to just settle for the default life. In the animal kingdom, creatures follow instinctual patterns from birth to death. Humans, however, possess the unique ability to learn, think and adapt, shaping their lives according to their desires. Nature didn't intend for us to merely exist.

You have the freedom to create your own purpose and leave a meaningful legacy. By following your passions and utilizing your thinking power, you can craft a fulfilling life filled with love and purpose, earning admiration from others in return.

Don't rush to label people. In a short story, the mother's observation of her daughters' behavior teaches a valuable lesson about snap judgments and the potential for growth in every individual.

Rather than labeling people based on limited actions, strive to understand their motivations and nurture open-mindedness. It's crucial to maintain boundaries and prioritize self-respect while treating others with kindness. True growth often requires letting go of toxic influences, even if initially uncomfortable, to pave the way for a brighter future.

Handling self when feeling completely down, it is unnecessary to get any motivation from outside. It lies in you. Create a list of past achievements titled "**My Wonders**" including educational accomplishments, contest wins, business ventures, mentoring successes, professional achievements, personal skills, and unique qualities. Reflecting on these successes instills positivity, fostering confidence to tackle challenges and get your energy back in your control.

"**Impacting at scale**" means making a profound difference in the lives of others through compassionate actions, aligning passionate work with supporting those in need. Your impactful value delivery should **positively influence and uplift numerous lives, in addition to your own success strategy.**

Can you make a difference to one's life? A girl throwing starfish one by one back into the ocean from the seashore. Surprised by this act, a man questioned, "there are so many on the shore, what it would make a difference."

She replied after throwing another one, "I made the difference to the life of that one fish" and she continued. This story emphasizes the importance of kindness and its ability to create positive change, inspiring us to make small differences wherever we can. This will give enormous fulfillment.

Forgiveness is essential for personal growth and success. By letting go of past failures and hurt, you free yourself from the weight of negativity that holds you back. **Start by forgiving yourself and then extend that forgiveness to others**. Holding onto grudges only hinders your progress and consumes your energy. Learn from experiences but choose to forgive and move forward with a renewed focus on your goals.

Chapter 4-Clarity-How to Choose a Topic: Key Takeaways

Losing focus on a selected topic is common diseases. Not only interest but valuable time fall into the trap of distraction due to other attractions. We select another topic and this cycle repeats. It is important to understand the reason before it is too late.

Most of the time, we choose any topics based on the influence of the trend or hype in the external environmental attraction. Alternatively, if the topic chosen is based on intrinsic motivation, then it is your real passion. Once done, real life starts, and it enables us to stay focused despite distractions.

Here, there were ten different techniques explained to identify your passion. So, before starting exercise, settle into a peaceful environment and your high productive time, to maximize focus. With a clear mind, recall moments of profound satisfaction or happiness, jotting them down under the column titled "My Passion." Next, delve into childhood memories, unearthing aspirations and inspirations that may have faded over time. Just capture it as well.

As you continue, reflect on unforeseen challenges you've confronted and how you navigated through them. Consider the lessons learned and the potential to share these insights with others through structured programs or online coaching. Tap into your areas of expertise, whether technical skills or leadership abilities, to develop impactful solutions or training programs.

Finally, revisit a long list of aspirations or life goals that may have been sidelined by circumstance, brainstorming small actionable steps to reignite their pursuit. Through this process of reflection, ideation and choosing the right topic to start with priority, you'll unearth a wealth of potential avenues to explore in pursuit of your life dream project.

Passionate leaders like Steve Jobs, Dr. A.P.J. Abdul Kalam, Ratan Tata, Robert Bosch, and Henry Ford are driven by noble causes, reflecting a deep commitment to improving lives. They exemplify the importance of a strong "why" behind their endeavors, with service and innovation as core motivations.

Their pursuit of noble causes brings them fulfillment and joy, with profit and recognition being mere side effects of their impactful work. Determine to become an influencing leader or businessperson, "to speak for voiceless" and there you will find your new you!

The research study conducted by Nash and Stevenson highlights the insufficiency of our understanding of fulfillment and success from a psychological perspective. They propose a framework comprising happiness, achievement, significance, and legacy as essential components of fulfillment, emphasizing the importance of hitting on all four categories for lasting satisfaction. Ultimately, the key lies in delivering value, uplifting others, and making a positive impact on people's lives.

Establishing authenticity through branding is crucial, be it for products or individuals. Without a unique brand, hard work might go unnoticed, as seen in my personal experiences.

Identity forms the core of personal branding, shaping actions and outcomes. Darren Gold [5] highlights how identity distinguishes average from exceptional performance, citing Muhammad Ali's bold self-proclamation as "king of the world." Embracing a chosen identity aligned with desired outcomes is emphasized for personal growth and success.

Chapter 5-Setting up Internal Infrastructure: Key Takeaways

In order to play soccer match, a good stadium is needed. Similarly, it is imperative to construct a solid mental infrastructure before diving into the game of life. Here is the step-by-step process to prepare your mindset involves recognizing the importance of mental preparation, breaking pattern for more creativity, taking breaks for better brain function, incorporating healthy habits like sleep and exercise, practicing digital detox, and creating a systematic approach to goal achievement.

To foster creativity and improve risk taking ability, break few routine patterns. Engage the brain with simple training that form **new neural pathways**. Start by exploring alternative routes to familiar destinations, memorizing new sights along the way.

Try to notice the curiosity and satisfaction that comes with discovering new paths, which will strengthen the brain's ability to adapt and change. Additionally, often try out with any small new activity introduced consistently activities like changing to new paste, learning to brush with left hand, start cycling, new exercise, learning a new language etc., These small steps will further develop cognitive abilities and boost confidence in all activities.

Pause to create idle moments for the brain. This Idle mode is called Brain's default function mode. During this time, **it tries to make new neurons connection**.

It is a wonderful exercise to get out of box ideas. Find a peaceful space, preferably in the morning, to sit, focus on breath sound and feel fresh oxygen energies each part of your body. Gradually increase the duration up to 10 or 15 minutes. This gives great energy and new thoughts.

To get an instant relief from evil thoughts, follow this exercise: Visualize a glowing candle and release negative emotions into its flame. Each emotional burden will disappear like smoke from a flame, leaving you with a sense of relief. Regularly practice these techniques to maintain mental freedom and emotional well-being.

14 approaches to prepare your mindset to achieve success are explained here. Preparing your mindset is more important than executing to stay consistent, it's crucial to understand your goals and devise actionable plans to achieve them. Taking regular breaks is essential for refreshing your brain and maintaining focus. Adopting a systematic approach with discipline ensures better results, similar to preparing for a sports match.

Breaking down your goals into achievable milestones and adhering to your own rules fosters consistency and progress. Focus solely on your chosen goal to avoid distractions and stay on track. Starting with small steps and maintaining consistency is key, even when feeling demotivated.

Visualizing success and finding intrinsic motivation are vital for staying motivated in the long run. Additionally, sharing goals partially can create positive pressure and accountability, while celebrating milestones and self-rewarding helps to maintain energy and motivation throughout the journey.

***

Could you please leave a review on the book?

One last time! I'd love if you could leave a review about the book. Reviews may not matter to big-name authors; but they're a tremendous help for authors like me, who don't have much following, and this is my very first book.

They help me to grow my readership by encouraging folks to take a chance on my books. To put it straight– reviews are the life blood for any author. **It is the sole means of connecting you and me**. Please leave your review by clicking the link below, it will directly lead you to the book review page.

PLEASE VISIT DIRECT CUSTOMER REVIEW LINK OF "*WIN INSIDE TO WIN OUTSIDE*"

It will just take less than a minute of yours but will tremendously help me to reach out to more people, so please leave your review. Thank you for supporting my work and I'd love to see your review of the book.

Short Preview of My Upcoming Book in this Self Improvement Mastery Series

---

THE POWER OF iDOING!
The Action Blueprint

In the **Self Improvement Mastery** series, we delve deep into the **art of taking action** and **turning ideas into reality**. This new upcoming book is designed to guide individuals toward mastering the art of execution and achieving meaningful transformation

This book is designed for those ready to break free from indecision and embrace a proactive mindset. You'll discover **practical strategies** to overcome barriers, harness your creativity, and execute your plans with confidence.

Through real-world examples and actionable insights, we will explore how ordinary individuals transformed their lives by embracing *The Power of intelligent Doing!* Whether you're an aspiring entrepreneur or someone seeking personal growth, this book will guide you in achieving sustainable success and fulfilment.

Join me on this journey to unlock your potential and learn how to transform your ideas into impactful actions. Let's master the art of execution together!

Chapter 1: Introduction
****

"The way to get started is to quit talking and begin doing"

– Walt Disney

The Engineer and the Broken Machine

A large manufacturing plant had a critical machine that suddenly broke down, halting all production. The company's mechanics tried everything they could to fix it, but nothing worked. Each hour the machine was offline, the company lost thousands of dollars.

Desperate, the factory owner called in a retired engineer who was known for his problem-solving skills. The engineer arrived with a small toolbox and quietly observed the machine for a few minutes. He then took a hammer, gently tapped one specific part, and the machine roared back to life.

The factory owner was relieved and asked the engineer for his bill. The engineer handed him an invoice for $10,000.

"Ten thousand dollars?!" the owner exclaimed. "You were here for only five minutes and all you did was tap the machine with a hammer. I need a detailed breakdown of this bill!"

The engineer smiled and wrote a new invoice:

- Tapping with a hammer: $1
- Knowing where to tap: $9,999

The moral of the story is action is important, but action with intelligent bring value to life. Action is about knowing *what* to do, *when* to do it, and *how* to do it. It's not just the effort you put in but the knowledge and skill behind that effort. Success often comes from precise, informed actions rather than blind hard work.

Act Now: Transform Ideas into Reality

We live in a sophisticated world shaped by the actions of millions of people who didn't just dream up ideas but executed them. If those ideas had remained just thoughts, we wouldn't enjoy the conveniences and technologies we have today.

Unfortunately, many ideas die in the ideation phase because of the fear of imperfection or mindset issues. It's not about whether an idea is good or bad—it's about execution. Even small ideas can lead to revolutionary changes, like the invention of the USB. Though simple, it created a massive impact on how we store and transfer data.

Without execution, ideas remain stagnant. In fact, many ideas evolve into bigger, more transformative concepts during the execution phase. Apple's iPhone, for instance, the iPhone wasn't the first invention of its kind. Phones, music players, and internet browsers existed long before. What set the iPhone apart was its ability to combine all these functions into a single, seamless device.

Through step-by-step execution and innovation, Apple transformed these individual technologies into a revolutionary product—the iPhone, which redefined the mobile industry.

Execution brought about this breakthrough, just as Jeff Bezos envisioned Amazon as more than an e-commerce platform. Cloud computing was already an idea, but it was Amazon's execution, with a well-structured plan, that turned Amazon Web Services (AWS) into a game-changing product.

Today, AWS powers thousands of companies worldwide, revolutionizing digital operations. Similarly, 3M's accidental creation of Post-it Notes became a global success through execution. These examples show how execution can transform a simple idea into something far more impactful.

Execution Fuels Innovation

Taking action is what drives us to innovate. Execution keeps the momentum going, pushing us to ask, "What's next?" and propelling the next step of innovation.

Consider Netflix: it began as a DVD rental service in 1997 but, through continual execution, evolved into the world's leading streaming service. Netflix's growth, from its humble beginnings to a company with over $31.6 billion in revenue, proves that execution unlocks the potential for transformation.

The company didn't have this future in mind when it started; clarity came through consistent action, especially as technology advanced.

This demonstrates the fundamental truth: ideas alone don't bridge the gap between intention and results. Only action does. In my own experience working in automotive software development, extensive real-world testing has always been essential after simulation environment testing.

Bridging the Gap Between Intention and Results

Execution is the only way to turn intention into tangible results. Planning may lay the groundwork, but the journey of execution often reveals unexpected challenges and opportunities.

Nike's famous slogan, "Just Do It," is a powerful example of the transformative power of action. In the late 1980s, Nike needed a fresh slogan to inspire people to take action, and "Just Do It" was born. This phrase, attributed to Dan Wieden of the advertising agency Wieden + Kennedy, perfectly encapsulates the importance of acting now, regardless of fear or hesitation. Today, it continues to motivate millions to pursue their goals with determination and grit.

What This Book Can Offer You?

This book is your guide to mastering the art of execution. It's for every growth-oriented individual who wants to turn ideas into results, achieve sustainable success, and live a life that leaves a legacy of inner fulfilment. It will help you avoid the regret of unfulfilled potential—because an idea that isn't acted upon is as good as no idea at all.

True joy comes from achieving milestones on the path to your larger goals. Every moment spent executing your passionate task brings a sense of accomplishment, like an artist immersed in their creation. When you focus on execution, time fades away, and all that matters is the task at hand.

In this book, you'll learn to:

- **How to take smart action to turn from a consumer mindset to a creator mindset.**
- **Action to Unlock the secret to fulfilment and lasting success.**
- **Turn challenges into opportunities.**
- **Boost your productivity.**

- **Master 16 key secrets for successful execution.**
- **Discover your inner action source for innovation and creativity.**
- **Achieve overall well-being and inner harmony through execution.**

Welcome aboard to discover *"THE TRUE POWER OF i(ntelligent) DOING!"*

Note: This book hits the shelves by Nov/2024. 😊

Copyright © 2024 by Azarudeen MJ. All rights reserved. No part of this book may be reproduced in any form without permission in writing from the author. No part of this publication may be reproduced or transmitted in any form or by any means, mechanical or electronic, including photocopying or recording, or by any information storage and retrieval system, or transmitted by email or by any other means whatsoever without permission in writing from the author.

Referral links:

[2] https://www.motortrend.com/features/top-10-greatest-american-cars-of-all-time/
[3] https://newsinhealth.nih.gov/2021/04/good-sleep-good-health
[4] https://www.business-standard.com/article/news-ians/kalam-concerned-about-disabled-developed-lightweight-prosthetics-115072801304_1.html
[5] https://www.forbes.com/sites/forbescoachescouncil/2019/05/21/the-power-of-identity/?sh=68eb5d923adf
[6] https://the-happy-manager.com/article/personal-development-stories/
[9] Research source: Success that lasts: https://consensus.app/papers/success-lasts-nash/662e532f17c75365aec707e5a8d61f18/
[10] https://parikshitjobanputra.com/where-there-is-a-will-there-is-always-a-way/
[11] https://asana.com/resources/limiting-beliefs

www.ingramcontent.com/pod-product-compliance
Lightning Source LLC
Chambersburg PA
CBHW052257220526
45471CB00001B/375